Business and Technology Integration

Integration for Success

Thomas Monte

ISBN: 1-4700-9955-1
ISBN-13: 9781470099558

dedication: To my wife, Carlota Masinsin-Monte, who has always loved and supported me.

CONTENTS

Chapter 1
Introduction

This book is a broad overview of the relationship between information technology and the business that it supports. It gives readers an overview of how information technology departments work, how to manage information technology departments, and how to build successful relationships with the business. In addition, there is a great deal of advice on a career in information technology. I have had three major career changing events in my career that changed the way I view information technology.

The first event was when I graduated from college at SUNY Plattsburgh with a degree in history and a minor in philosophy. My career plan was eventually to become a history professor. I tried teaching with my father for a brief period, but the job was not a good fit for me. It was merely by luck that I fell into the field of information technology. While I was trying to find some direction, I accepted a job working on a help desk. I had very limited exposure to technology at the time and was curious. I remember thinking it would be a growing field in the mid-nineties. What followed was the dotcom boom. While I worked at the help desk, I learned about technology and made the decision to pursue a career in technology. While I was establishing my career, my mother was looking for a career change. I suggested that she switch into technology as well. My mother is now working for Intel and has a successful established career. The first lesson I learned is that technology is, for the most part, a meritocracy, and anyone who is dedicated and willing to work hard can succeed.

Once I realized I wanted to pursue a career in information technology, I set about the task of learning exciting cutting-edge technology. The problem was that I had just graduated from college and did not have any money. I decided to take a risk and invest in my career. I bought an Acer Pentium 90 desktop for $3,000. This was a massive sum of money for me at the time because I was only making about $14,000 a year. Every night after work, I tinkered with my computer and Microsoft Windows 3.11. I also participated in the beta for Windows 95 and was amazed at the transformative impact of the new interface and features. It was around this time when I met the company network administrator, who was running a Novell network. I decided that I wanted to learn about networks and Novell. I did some research and discovered I could achieve certification in Novell administration. I signed up for a class to become a Certified Novell Administrator or CNA and spent another $3,000. After I passed the exam, I got another job making almost double, what I was making before. The wizards on Wall Street are lucky to make 10 percent on an investment and I had doubled my money in a few months! This money was not just a bonus it was a salary increase. Salary increases are compound interest. Compound interest is essentially the interest you make on interest. An example will help clarify how it works. Let us say you make $50,000 a year and you receive a 3 percent raise. The raise would be $1,500 and the new salary would be $51,500. If you receive another raise the next year at 3 percent, you would get a raise of $1,545. If you compare the raise for the first year and the second year, you would make $45 just from the 3 percent interest and your new salary would be $53,045. When you consider a career can easily be forty years, the compound interest quickly adds up. If you get big raises early in your career, the compound interest over the course of your career adds up to a significant amount of money. The second lesson is never stop investing in your career. I have never lost money investing in my career or education.

The third event was about ten years later after I had been in information technology for some time. I was shocked to receive a poor performance review. I had a very tough year with long hours, late nights, and a number of impressive technical accomplishments. I realized my problem was a failure of interpersonal relationships and a failure to treat my job like a business. I promised myself that I would fix both issues. It was not easy, but over the next several years, I was able to transform myself from what I like to call a technology professional into a business technology professional. Technology professionals are only concerned with technology. Business technology professionals look at how technology can support the business. Business technology professionals are providing a service. The third lesson is your job exists to serve a business need. Information technology professionals should see themselves as not only information technology professionals, but business and customer service professionals as well.

In addition to my personal epiphanies, I had inadvertently learned about private enterprise. My journey started in Buffalo, New York, but it took me all over the world. I never turned down an opportunity to travel. I worked in New York, New Jersey, Pennsylvania, New Mexico, California, and in many other states. I also traveled internationally to the United Kingdom and the Philippines. I worked at a large variety of companies from small companies of fifty people all the way up to international Fortune 500 companies with thousands of employees. I have also worked in a wide variety of sectors from financials to telecommunications. Ironically, in all of those experiences I saw companies repeating the same mistakes. If I had to sum up the main problem, it would be that information technology departments and business units often do not understand each other, communicate, or efficiently coordinate. The relationship is usually more like a divorced couple living in the same house passing each other in the hall.

Over the years, I have mentored family, friends, and coworkers sharing my insights about technology and business. This book is a natural extension of that advice and a chance to reach a wider audience. While I was writing this book, I had three broad groups of readers in mind. When I was stuck on how to tackle an issue or topic, I tried to remember these three business perspectives. What does a first-time information technology manager need to know? What does an information technology professional need to know? What should business professionals know about technology? I found by asking myself the questions that the book really wrote itself in a much shorter period than I expected! I have highlighted below what I hope the different groups of readers will get out of this book.

First Time Information Technology Managers

The most targeted group and probably the people that will be most interested in this book are first-time information technology managers. When I accepted my first management job, I knew that my responsibilities would change. I had changed my technology role many times over the years. My familiar pattern was to read books, gain certification, and fill in gaps on the job. The pattern had served me well. I bought books and read up on managing, but I found that there was not much good advice in many of them. I also researched certifications and there are not many of those either, unless you want get a business degree, which would take years. This left me with my last option of learning on the job. I also thought I had a secret weapon in what I had already learned. I think we have all been in a position with a boss that made decisions that made you want to pull your hair out and thought, "I wouldn't do it that way." My first management job was a humbling experience. I quickly learned how different management and technical employee roles are from each other. While I would like to think I have improved a great deal as a manager, I still have a lot of work to do. If I had to guess, I would say that my experience is not that different from most other first time managers. In hindsight, there were several big mistakes in my calculations. Management and Technology jobs are as different as switching from construction to medicine. They are a completely different set of skills. Managers need to hire, manage, terminate, create and track budgets, give performance reviews, plan projects, and performs many other tasks. Most employees never have to do any of those tasks. However, my technical training was not a waste of time. When you are dealing with the subject matter of technology, your background will be invaluable in making sound technical decisions. The second big change is that most technical problems are binary problems. Success is obvious, straightforward and black and white. When you are managing people, success is more ambiguous. I have walked away many times from a situation as a manager with no idea if I made the right decision. This is a frustrating thing about being a manager. This book will help readers who are new to management learn some new techniques that make the transition to management less painful.

Information Technology Professionals

When I was an employee, I often wondered how and why a company made decisions, especially the ones I would not have made. In addition to satisfying your curiosity, information technology professionals will gain other benefits from this book. It will give them a broad overview of how information technology departments work. If you are thinking of switching into another department, the technology sections will give you some insight into how those groups work and what challenges they face. The business sections will help prepare you for more business related duties that may be outside your comfort zone. It can also help you decide, if you really want to stay in technology or move into management.

Business Professionals

Business professionals will gain the most insight from learning how information technology departments work from the first half of the book. Business professionals may not get as much from the second half of the book. I am hoping business professionals that read my book will talk to the information technology department afterward. They may learn a new way to leverage technology to support the business. I also hope business professionals see how dedicated and passionate information technology professionals. I know many people in the field that work well over forty hours and then go home and study or work in a practice lab on their own time. Information technology professionals are some of the most dedicated people in the world to there craft.

Organization of this Book

There are always sacrifices in trying to reach a broad group of readers while at the same time covering a broad scope of topics. I included useful details without going too deeply into any one topic. Each section has its unique tradeoffs, but this strikes a good balance that will allow most readers to benefit from each chapter.

The technical sections focus on the various fields of information technology: help desk, desktop support, server operations and engineering, network engineering, information security, and audit. Each specialization is broken down exactly the same way with an introduction, tools, teams, and hiring, tactical challenges, strategic challenges, and conclusions. The hiring sections cover hiring specifically related to the skills for that technical specialization. Hiring also has a separate chapter. In case you have not noticed, I consider hiring an important topic and devote a significant number of pages to it. Challenges are broken down into tactical and strategic. Tactical challenges are the short-term problems a group faces. Strategic challenges are the long-term problems a department faces as yearly goals. The conclusion wraps up final thoughts on the group.

The business chapters are not as formulaic, and each chapter has a unique structure around the topic presented. Furthermore, the business sections are less specific, as well, for two reasons. First, I am a business technology professional. I had a school-of-hard-knocks education in management skills. I learned what I know from work experience and the CISSP, PMP, and ITIL certifications. There are some benefits and drawbacks, but I can only write what I know so this is what I have to share on those topics. Second, I wanted to give technology professionals basic commonsense tips on management skills. As a result, many of the discussions and charts are significantly less complex than a real analysis would be to make the concepts clear. Readers can take the concepts and adapt them to their unique circumstances. The more detailed and thoughtful your analysis is the more likely it will achieve results for you.

I avoid talking about specific products as much as possible; however, in some cases where there is a clear market leader, it was unavoidable. Microsoft and Cisco are dominant in their respective markets. There are several advantages to this approach. First, the book stands a better chance of standing the test of time. Second, I am more interested in teaching concepts than concrete solutions. This book is about giving you tools to adapt to your specific situation. Often I present a concept in one section that you can apply to other areas of information technology and business. If you learn something in one information technology area, figure out if you can apply the concept to another area.

Chapter 2
HELP DESK

Introduction

The help desk is usually the face of the information technology department to employees, executives, and customers. The United Kingdom and ITIL publications call the help desk the service desk. However, for purposes of this chapter, I will refer to it as the help desk. The purpose of a help desk is to solve customer problems as efficiently as possible. This means using the lowest cost option to solve any given problem.

The method consists of receiving tickets from customers and tracking them to completion. The help desk may assign tickets to other departments, but the help desk is responsible for the ticketing system, providing updates and closing tickets. George Santayana said, "Those who cannot remember the past are condemned to repeat it."[1] There are few places this is more true than any given company's policy on a ticketing system. Companies that do not consistently use a ticketing system use multiple systems, or worse, no system, suffer repeatedly from the same issues. Companies that live and die by the ticketing system rarely repeat the same mistake twice.

While bureaucracy is efficient most of the time, it can sometimes lead to frustration and poor service when an unexpected problem comes up. This chapter describes several ways to compensate and minimize these issues. There are also challenges working on the help desk. The help desk is usually the lowest level job in information technology and sometimes the whole company; because of that fact sometimes other employees, management and customers treat them poorly. When I was a kid growing up in Buffalo, my father would take me to work with him. My father was an inner-city gym teacher, and I always looked forward to going to work with him. Every time I went, I would have a good time and learned something new. When I was about ten, I went in with him, and he stopped to talk to the janitor. He spent about ten minutes talking to the janitor, telling jokes, offering to do him several favors, and fussing over the guy in general. When he walked away, I asked my father why he spent so much time with the janitor when he was a teacher and obviously more important. He told me "Tom, that guy is the most important person in the building."

I responded, "How can that be? Isn't the principle the most important?"

My father laughed and replied, "The principle isn't going to clean or leave the gym open late." My father is a very wise man. The most important person is not always the one with the most important title. This has proven true many times in my career. Plenty of times an assistant, janitor, or a help desk person helped me solve a problem.

Many years later, I was providing technical support directly to the CEO at a large company. He was having a problem with his e-mail, and his executive assistant was working with me to fix it. I determined that I needed help to resolve the problem. The company e-mail administrator was a mean, difficult person to work with. She had yelled at me on the phone several times and I did not like dealing with her. I called her up on speakerphone with the CEO's assistant on the phone and told her a user was having a problem. I did not tell her who the user was. She began screaming and cursing at us. The CEO's assistant cut her off and told her who she was and whose e-mail was having a problem. The CEO's executive assistant hung up and immediately called the vice president of information technology. The e-mail administrator called me back about ten minutes later, profusely apologizing for her behavior. If the e-mail administrator had treated us better, she could have saved herself from an embarrassing situation and one that, in some companies, could have led to termination. The more important lesson is that if she treated everyone better, she would not have to worry about it.

When I became a director, I learned another way to apply this lesson. Directors deal with internal company politics over employees, time with executive management, money, and backing when there is an issue between departments. If you misjudge how to deal with another manager, you could end up in a situation that costs you your job. It can reveal the character of the person you are dealing with. If they treat those people poorly, how are they going to treat me? What will they say behind my back?

The two lessons about the help desk are that the ticketing system is a mission critical application in every company and everyone should treat everyone with respect.

Tools
Phone System or Chat
The help desk provides the first level of support for the customers of information technology services. The help desk can be informal in a small company or complex and sophisticated in a large company. Traditionally, employees provide support by telephone. The company usually provides an 800 number and options to reach the right group. Phone systems should have at least a limited phone menu, a way to track call statistics, and a way to record calls. If you decide to automate the initial call, make sure the phone menu does not take long to get through. A pet peeve of mine is the automated system asking for my account information and then the person on the line asking for it again. Chat support is gaining traction and becoming a more popular tool. I personally prefer chat, but some people prefer to call in. I expect video chat will become common with the prevalence of video chat and webcams. Chat systems need to be able to record the session like a phone conversation and provide easy access for customers.

Ticketing Systems

The ticketing system solves multiple business problems at the same time. First, the ticketing system gives a company a single point of reference for all issues so they can prioritize them and deal with them in order according to their respective importance. If you do not organize all your issues in one place, it is difficult to set priorities. Second, the ticketing system provides a record of past issues that an employee can reference for solutions to future problems. If the top technical minds in your company have a place to post solutions and close issues, your first line of help-desk support can identify and solve those issues in the future rather than continuing to tie up those technical minds. Third, a ticketing system produces metrics. Metrics are a measure of the current state of something. Once you have a collection of metrics, you can create a baseline. A baseline is a trend identified by a collection of metrics. Once you have a baseline, you will be able to identify patterns. Use this information to identify common issues and employee performance. If you cannot measure a problem, it is impossible to solve it. Here are two small charts that illustrate the power of metrics. Company A produced the following two charts from the ticketing system for last month.

Priority Chart

Priority	Tickets
Critical	20
High	30
Medium	50
Low	200
Total	300

This chart shows us the majority of the tickets are low-priority tickets. However, we also see there were fifty critical and high tickets. This company clearly has stability issues, or they are not prioritizing tickets correctly. If this company can solve this problem, they can provide much more stable and responsive support. However, we also want to know what is happening with the low-priority tickets. The next chart looks at the breakdown within the low-priority tickets. You should use this same process to look at the medium, high and critical tickets.

Low Ticket Breakdown

Low Tickets	Category
Password Reset	100
Printer Problem	83
Software Update	15
Mouse or Keyboard	2

The breakdown of the low tickets shows us that if we can provide an automated solution to password resets, we can cut the average monthly calls to the help desk in half. This would be a huge improvement in efficiency. If a company does not have automatic password resets, this is frequently the most common call to the help desk. If you spend ten minutes on every password reset and you remove all one hundred tickets, you are saving 1,000 minutes or over sixteen hours per month of time for the help desk. If you are paying people on the help desk $20 per hour, you saved the company $333 per month. If there are costs to the password reset solution, you would need to factor those into your calculations, but the value of having this information should be obvious. You may be able to find solutions to other categories of tickets.

A good ticketing system should have the following features.

1. Accountability—You create accountability by assigning tickets, and if you hold people accountable for getting them done, results will follow. The help desk should assign all tickets in the system and solve them or escalate them to another team. The help desk remains responsible for tracking, getting updates, and making sure tickets are closed.

2. Ticket tracking—Every ticket needs a unique identifier so the ticket can be referenced by customers and internal employees. This allows you to maintain a history of the ticket, provide updates, and close them when the person who reported them states they are complete.

3. Reporting—The ticketing system should have the ability to generate reports for management. The reports should be able to show a wide range of metrics from the average time it takes to close a ticket to what the most common categories of tickets are. The priority section below will give you an idea about what these reports should look like.

4. Priorities—The system needs the capability to assign priorities so that if fifty tickets come in at the same time, you know which ones to address first. In addition, you know how quickly to address them.

There are two ways to measure the impact of an issue on a business. Quantitative priorities are priorities that you can easily measure, like how many people or services are affected. However, the priorities of some issues require more than the number of people affected. For example, if the CEO were working on a merger with a deadline, obviously any issue he encounters would be a high priority for any information technology department. This is a qualitative priority or judgment call. If you take these two criteria together, you can accurately assess the impact of any issue. When you add the quantitative priority and the qualitative priority together, they become the priority level. Priority levels are urgent, high, medium, and low. If you note the last row, it is labeled escalation time. Some tickets will sit in a queue indefinitely for a variety of reasons. All open tickets need to get resolved, even if they are low priority. The best way to make sure that happens is by gradually raising the priority on tickets. Eventually, low tickets will become high or urgent tickets where they will get resolved. Here is a generic sample chart of ticketing system priorities.

	Urgent	High	Medium	Low
Qualitative Impact	Business critical components, data center outage, or major site down	Multiple employees down or performance degraded	One to three employees affected, but there is a work around available	Single employee affected
Quantitative Impact	Major impact to the business	Minor impact to the business	Minimal impact to the business	Insignificant impact to the business
Staff	Entire IT department informed, and any resources necessary are immediately involved	Ticket is escalated to second level of help desk support for assessment	Next available help desk person	Next available help desk person
Response Time	Immediate	30 minutes	Business hours	Business hours
Escalation Time	Senior management notified of updates	1 day	5 days	10 days

If your company does not have a set of priorities, you can modify the chart to your business needs. You should also make the escalation time row more generous until the teams involved adjust to the process. Once you have your chart, you need to get company buy in. You should meet with and take suggested improvements from your manager, the business units you support, and executive management. Once your new standard has approval, you need to launch a campaign to educate the company and customers about the policy and to explain the requirements.

When I introduced this process at a company that did not have it, information technology started to get a more positive reputation for being responsive. The business immediately became easier to work with and the information technology team had known expectations about when they needed to solve problems. Everyone knew what to expect from each other, and that was what had been missing. Another way to describe what we did was an OLA or operating level agreement. We had a formal joint agreement on the service the information technology organization would provide. Service level agreement or SLAs are levels of service with customers. In addition to the charts, I held regular weekly meetings with the business to go over metrics and lingering problems. This further reinforced that we were supporting our internal and external customers and gave them an opportunity to raise issues. These meetings were sometimes uncomfortable, but they paid off in respect and more trust from the business.

However, a handful of individual employees were unhappy with the change. The OLA or SLA makes sure the company addresses the most important business needs first and provide an agreed upon level of support. When you do not have a formal process in place, usually the people who scream loudest gets his or her problem resolved first. These employees saw that their issues were no longer the high priority. It is also difficult for employees and customers to understand that when they cannot work, it may not be the business's top priority. However, if one user is unable to work with one problem and one hundred users can't work due to another problem, information technology needs to focus resources on the problem affecting more users or higher priority. In addition, information technology should not have to drop all of its project work for issues that affect a single user. Whenever a user was dissatisfied with the service, they were able to call me directly as the manager responsible for information technology operations. If you are an internal information technology department, you need feedback from the business. If you do not talk to your internal clients, they will be talking to your boss eventually. User frustration can be a difficult balancing act. Sometimes you need to raise the priority on issues that really do not deserve it for the sake of good public relations. It takes time to develop a balance between priorities, your team, and providing good customer service. There are no easy answers, but open communication between the business and technology gives you an opportunity to get it right.

Documentation
The help desk should have current documentation and training available for themselves and the users they support. Good user documentation will allow users to solve simple problems and configurations without the intervention of the help

desk. The best way to test documentation is to ask someone uninvolved with the process to work through the directions. A good detail-oriented tester will help you refine your documentation.

Teams

A help desk team provides several different levels of support. In case you did not notice, I am treating the automated phone system as an employee of the team. This is not by accident. In a large company, an automated phone system can act as an additional employee by directing calls, accepting payment, activating credit cards, and so on.

Level 0-Automated Systems

Automated systems are any technology that a company can activate to provide support without human intervention. This could be a web page, a phone system IVR, or a document that a system e-mails to employees. While smart use of automated support can make information technology cost effective, avoid becoming too automated and losing touch with your customers. When a help-desk team reported to me, I regularly sent out surveys and met with users to make sure I understood day-to-day concerns. It also helps to address a few tickets yourself so you stay familiar with the process and users.

Level 1-The Front Lines

The first level of help desk support are the first people you speak with. Since the help desk's goal is to solve problems as cheaply as possible, the first person you speak to will have access to common problems and solutions. If the problem goes beyond common solutions, that person will usually escalate it to the next level of support. It annoys me when I cannot directly talk to the second and third level of escalation. I find this condescending. If the help desk escalates an issue, the customer should be able to speak directly to the person helping him or her. It is more efficient and provides a better customer experience.

Level 2-Technical Experts

The second level of help desk support is usually help desk employees that have worked on the help desk for a while or members of the desktop or server teams. They know all the common solutions that the first level of support can provide, and they know about old issues and probably have a few tricks they can try.

Level 3-Senior Technical Experts and Managers

If you have reached this level, you probably have a difficult problem on your hands. Depending on the company, this level is either the most senior technical people or managers that can work with you to find alternative solutions.

Hiring

We talk about hiring in general in a separate chapter, but here we focus on what to look for specifically in help desk employees. When you are looking for help desk employees, the most important skill is good customer service. I would rather hire someone with no technical experience and good customer service skills over someone who is highly technical for a help desk position. It is easy to teach technical skills and difficult to teach good customer service skills. Because most help desks operate on a shift basis, make sure up front that candidates can work the hours you need them.

Tactical Challenges

The most common tactical challenge is employee turnover. Many companies simply accept the high level of turnover and miss a great opportunity for themselves and their employees. If you have a good employee working on a help desk, why would you want to lose the investment and a person that you know does a good job? Companies should make aggressive efforts to retain and promote good, hard-working people. The desktop support team is a natural transition for someone working on the help desk. A good way to let help desk people know they have a future in the company is to allow them to spend a day in several of the other teams to help and learn what they do.

Some managers believe you should not promote or train employees. They believe employees will leave with the investment you made in them. My counter argument is that if you do not give your best people opportunities for advancement, they will leave anyway. The least productive employees will stay because they have nowhere else to go. When you give one person a promotion out of the help desk, or any department for that matter, you have motivated everyone in the department to do a better job. Employees in the department will see the company values them and they have an opportunity at promotions and better pay. It will no longer feel like a dead end. Companies would gain employee loyalty, higher productivity, and save money by avoiding the constant churn of training new employees.

Internal promotion does not just apply to the help desk. I have never stopped anyone from leaving any team I managed. In fact, I encourage any team I manage to share their career goals with me. Ultimately, employees will leave your team eventually anyway. Why not be open, honest, and make it a more pleasant experience for everyone? In addition to being good for morale, I like to help people. You also never know when someone who worked for you will hit it big and hire you to be the CIO. I am still waiting for that to happen.

Strategic Challenges

The three major challenges for the help desk are the ticketing system, documentation, and call management.

As we discussed, the ticketing system is critical to any company. The ticketing system is the backbone of the help-desk team. A good help desk team will obsess over the ticketing system and make sure the rest of the company is aware of the value it brings. Management should support the help desk and enforce the ticketing system for all requests and incidents.

A common problem in all areas of technology is a lack of documentation or updated documentation. You will see documentation as a recurring theme that I harp on throughout the book. Technical people usually see documentation as a waste of time. Most technical people feel there is no value to a task unless they are doing something technical. The way I see it, documentation saves significant amounts of time. Imagine that you write a set of instructions, and it takes you one hour to write and distribute the instructions. If you save six people ten minutes, the time you spent paid for itself. If you are out of the office, the time spent documenting the instructions could be worth far more to you. The company can still function and you can enjoy your time off. Unfortunately, it takes time to see the benefits of documentation, but it will pay off in the long run. You should have documentation that discusses escalation procedures, call trees, troubleshooting processes, and any other common tasks the help desk performs. Every team should have all the documentation anyone needs to perform any function or task within the team.

Call management is another critical part of the help desk function. How you handle call management is largely dependent on the size of the company and resources of the help desk. You should have, at a minimum, a web page with common issues and a phone number to call. A large organization should have a sophisticated self-help system and a phone system that routes calls to specific queues.

Conclusions

The help desk is all about communicating and coordinating customer support. The help desk is the central point of contact for managing, escalating, and reporting on all requests and issues. The help desk has the most direct interaction with customers. An effective help desk can provide a company with accurate issue reporting, escalations, and metrics for identifying recurring issues and gauging employee performance. The help desk needs to coordinate tickets with all the departments in information technology. The help desk should also provide metrics to management to gauge the performance of the information technology department.

CHapter 3
DESKTOP SUPPORT

Introduction

Desktop support is usually part of the help desk in smaller organizations and a separate department in larger organizations. The desktop support team builds and manages user desktops and laptops. Sometimes desktop support is also responsible for cell phone and desktop encryption key management.

A common issue is naming convention for laptops and desktops. This is important for servers and network devices as well. Many small companies name devices after users. For example, they might name Bob's laptop Bob. This works well while Bob is at the company, but if Bob leaves, you would need to change the name of the machine, remove Bob's information, and name it to the new user. While this may not seem like an important issue, I think it represents professionalism and attention to detail. It is embarrassing during an audit to explain why you call a critical server Ren or Stimpy. In addition to professionalism, the name can represent critical details about the device you are dealing with. Let us look at a sample naming convention to get a better understanding of how it would work.

Company: XX where Cerebellum Strategies, LLC could be CS

Location: XXX where Dallas could be DA1, assuming you have more than one location in Dallas.

Device Type: DES for Desktop, SRV for server, and so on

Number: XXX or 001

Resulting name: CSDA1DES001

Based on the name, you can tell the company, location, and device type. You have the flexibility to have up to 999 devices with this naming convention, but you could add more digits. This sample should give you some ideas for your company. If you are a hospital, you could add an L to the beginning of the name to any device that relates to patient life support. If an information-technology support professional were looking at the device remotely, he or she would know that special procedures are required for managing the device because a patient's life could be at stake. The naming scheme is equally important for servers and network devices that support equally critical business operations. Of course, knowing which devices are mission critical requires interaction with the business units, which is a frequent topic throughout this book.

Naming conventions also tie into another theme of consistency. The goal of each department in information technology should be to build devices like an assembly line. The fewer variations you have in devices, the easier they are to support.

It will no longer matter if someone in information technology has never logged into a device before because it will be exactly the same configuration as the last fifty devices that person worked on. Inconsistency is the enemy of efficiency at all levels of business. This is one of the key concepts of the book "The Visible Ops Handbook: Implementing ITIL in 4 Practical and Auditable Steps." I highly recommend this book to all information technology professionals. The book makes an in-depth, compelling case for consistency. Consistency does not just apply to processes. It is equally important in choosing hardware, server room setup, and so forth.

Tools

It is usually harder to convince a company to make an investment in the desktop team than it is get an investment for the help desk, server, or network teams. As a result, I have created very simple business justifications with a cost savings analysis and a risk based analysis. You can apply these two models to anything you want to purchase in information technology.

Imaging Software

The desktop team will need to configure desktops and laptops for new users, upgrades, and replacements. Imaging machines is a repetitive mind-numbing process. I used to provide desktop support at a small company of about fifty people. Every computer the company had was a different configuration, and the company wanted to replace 30 percent of the computers. I convinced them to replace all of the computers for two reasons. First, we were able to get a better discount. Second, I was able to create two images that both worked on every computer. This was extremely efficient. I could have a machine rebuilt in thirty minutes and it only required about five minutes of my time. It took some time to setup the initial image, but over the course of the life of the machines, I more than made my time back. I don't remember the specifics, but let's look at a reasonable example. If it takes you five hours or 300 minutes to create each image and roll out every device, you have spent 500 minutes to create the machines. It is reasonable to spend an hour building a machine for a total of fifty hours or 3,000 minutes. This would have saved you 2,500 minutes or about forty man-hours. If you are paying a desktop support person $20 per hour, you saved the company $800 minus the cost of imaging software and storage space. If you save $800 building fifty machines, imagine building 1,000 machines. Spending money on imaging software will save your company money in man-hours and time. You should look at every purchase from this perspective. What am I spending and what will I get in return? This makes it very easy to figure out which purchases are cost effective.

Imaging software has two other benefits. If a user is having a problem with a computer, you can take an image to save the user's data and configuration to apply to another machine. The last benefit is to save data when an employee leaves. This is particularly useful if the employee had business-critical information or the employee left under bad circumstances. Information security should always be involved in approving images and particularly in saving images the company may require for litigation. Security professionals should manage the process for taking images of machines that may be involved in litigation. Security professionals will know how to apply the rules for chain of custody. At a very basic level, chain of custody is proving that no one tampered with the evidence while it is collected and stored.

Application Management

The desktop team will need to roll out application updates, new applications, delete old applications, and track licensing. The same rules that apply to desktop imaging software also apply to application management. It also has the same business case. Involve information security in providing and approving updates.

Anti-Virus Enterprise Software

Anti-virus software has a different business case. As a result, how can you justify spending thousands of dollars on an enterprise anti-virus package? The business case for buying enterprise anti-virus software is the same reason people buy insurance. Insurance is all about managing risk. Risk is calculating the cost of a problem happening and how likely it is to happen. If one user gets a virus on a system, it can affect the rest of the company or even worse clients or partners. Every business should calculate how much it costs the business to lose its technology or Internet connection for periods of an hour, a day, or a week. Once a business invests in making the calculation, almost every technology decision becomes very easy. Let us assume the cost of an entire day outage will cost the company $50,000, and we believe the likelihood of a problem is 10 percent in any given year. The enterprise anti-virus package costs $4,000. A simple calculation of $50,000 x .10 = $5,000. Based on the risk, the enterprise anti-virus package is worth the risk. Involve the information security team in approving and validating the anti-virus systems and policies, and regularly update them.

Teams

Desktop support teams do not usually require many specialized skills, so most of the people in the team will have the same skill sets. It is important to make sure everyone on the team knows how to troubleshoot a problem, provide basic desktop support, and manage all of the desktop automation tools described in the previous system. In addition, the desktop team should tightly focus on the ticketing queues and watching for trends and opportunities to improve efficiency and educate the user base.

Hiring

Desktop teams require more technical skill than help desk positions, but customer service skills are even more important. When desktop support personnel need to interact with customers, they will usually be working in person. Desktop support personnel should have technical skills with the desktop operating system you are using. This is usually a PC with windows, but Apple computers and Linux machines are becoming more common. They should also have some experience with Microsoft Office products including Word, Excel, and PowerPoint.

Tactical Challenges

Desktop teams suffer from high turnover the same way help desk teams do. The best solution is internal promotion that we discussed in the last chapter. The most natural transition from the desktop team is to the server team or to a junior role in information security.

Strategic Challenges

The biggest strategic challenge for desktop teams is automation. A desktop team could manage one hundred devices for every employee in the department or more. In order to accomplish that feat, desktop support teams need to develop a high degree of automation to meet customer demand and keep software up to date.

Documentation is critical. Keep all processes and procedures documented and current. The litmus test of your documentation is to hire a new desktop support employee give them desktop support documentation. If they cannot perform the tasks, make it a priority to improve your documentation.

Conclusions

The desktop support team is all about automation, retention of employees, and documentation. Desktop support teams rely on the help desk to coordinate and resolve user issues. Desktop teams also work with server teams to make sure e-mail clients and file shares work. They are one of the most critical teams for the information security team to have a strong relationship with because users cause almost all information security issues. Involve information security in providing desktop encryption, security hardening, anti-virus protection, remote access, and data collection for litigation.

Chapter 4
SERVER SUPPORT AND ENGINEERING

Introduction

Server support and engineering manages the computers for multiple users to leverage services such as printers, file shares, web servers, fax, e-mail, DNS, and custom applications. I defined the roles of the server team as support and engineering. These are actually two separate skill sets, and two different personalities work best in each position. Server support is concerned with managing production servers and responding to outages. Server support works best for people who like excitement, working under pressure, and being active. Server engineering is concerned with planning and designing solutions for the business. People who like to plan things in advance and methodically calculate results work best in this role. It requires both skills to manage the server infrastructure of a company. You will also find the same break down between support and engineering in networking. The same people in the same team, different people in the same team, or completely separate teams may handle these roles. I recommend having two separate job roles within the same team. Most people work better in one role or the other, so it makes sense to separate the job functions. However, separate teams will create barriers to communication and coordination.

Server teams have fewer interactions directly with the business and customers. The help desk and desktop field most of the end user and customer support so that the server teams can focus on the servers. Server teams only get involved in support when there is a server outage, and even in those cases, the help desk and desktop support usually have the direct interaction. In keeping with the theme of this book, I think server engineers should meet with the business directly.

There are several reasons for direct communication between the server team and the business units. Server teams may not be fully aware of how the business uses its resources and which ones are most important. Whenever I sit down with a business unit for the first time I always learn something new that gives me ideas on how to improve the way information technology supports the business. These discussions could lead you to solutions like replacing a printer or adding redundancy to a service. Server team monitoring metrics can also become more focused as a result of these conversations. Even if you do not get any technical concrete results from the meeting, you are showing the business that you care. Almost every time I request a meeting with a business unit, they greet me with a warm reception and thank me profusely just for listening. It usually takes an hour or two to set up the meeting and follow up. This has been, without a doubt, some of the most productive time in my career. I would encourage every server engineer to speak to users and make improvements based on the feedback. This advice does not just apply to server teams; it works for every department and manager in IT. Effective business support requires that you understand the business.

Every server team should also provide reports and OLA/SLAs to the organizations they support. As we discussed earlier, OLAs and SLAs guarantee a levels of service. Every team I have worked with has shown an initial reluctance to providing reports and guaranteed service levels. I think most teams are concerned that reports will put them under more scrutiny and criticism. I see it differently. If you are doing a good job, you should get the recognition you deserve. One of the best ways to do that is to provide reports showing objectively what you have achieved. If you are doing poorly, the reports will tell you where to look to make improvements. Either way, you will improve the performance and perception of your team. The first step is to get a baseline. A baseline is a set of metrics that show where service is now. Generate an initial report and discuss it with your team and manager. Once you have agreement with information technology on the metrics, you should review the report. This will give you a chance to make improvements before you show the report to business units. For example, if a server is always using a large amount of memory, you may need to get a patch to fix the memory leak. However, if you have a hardware problem and need to upgrade or replace a server, this is where the monitoring really shines. You will be able to provide charts and measures illustrating the problem to management, rather than complaining with no substantiated justification.

Tools
Servers

Servers are the reason server teams exist and should be the core focus of everything the teams do. There are many options to choose from with servers.

- Rack mounted or stand-alone—You should have a rack, and properly mount your servers.
- Physical, blade, hosted, or cloud—Physical servers are servers you build and maintain. Blade servers are large machines that have slots for each physical server. Another company's data center handles hosted servers. Cloud servers are virtual servers hosted in the Internet.
- Single server or virtual—You can install one operating system on each server, or install virtualization software and install multiple virtual servers.
- Internal or external storage—The server can use internal hard drives or get its storage space from an external device, like a SAN or storage area attached network.

- Operating system—There is an almost endless list of server operating system choices from Microsoft Windows Server, Novell, Linux, OpenB- SD, Solaris, and many more. You should try to standardize on one or at most a couple of operating systems. The more operating systems you maintain, the more skill sets you need to manage them. You should make sure that your server team is intimately familiar with the operat- ing system and send your team to regular training.

Monitoring

Desktop monitor is a good tool to have, but for servers monitoring is critical to survival. You should monitor at least CPU, memory utilization, hard disk space, and network utilization. The help desk and server support should receive alerts on any unusual activity. Once you have those charts and metrics it is easy to proac- tively track down potential problems and fix them before they become a problem. In addition, you can use the reports to report SLA statistics to upper management. Once you have the metrics, the only way to benefit from them is to consistently and methodically look at them every day and track down the root cause of unusual metrics. Here are a few examples of what I typically look for.

- CPU—The CPU is the brain of the computer and will have a capacity that can go up to 100 percent. The CPU should stay below 50 percent with some spikes above that. If the server is below 10 percent CPU, you probably are not taking full advantage of the server.
- Memory—When memory stays above 80 percent utilization, you should investigate what is causing the utilization. This is a good indi- cator the server has a memory leak or an application that is continually taking more memory without releasing the memory it does not need.
- Hard drive space—When a server gets to 10 percent of disk space free, you should either delete files or add space otherwise the server will crash.
- Application monitoring—Monitor all ports and services that are criti- cal to the business. If you are monitoring a partner's IP address or the port your web server customers log into, you can get an alert and al- ready be working on the problem before your customers and clients call you. If you are going to monitor a partner or customer's network, you need to make sure you get permission first.

As with other areas, documentation is important to server support and engi- neering. Server support and engineering should have detailed inventories of each server it manages and documentation on how to build and update servers. A good test of the quality of the documentation is to pick a server at random, and ask the server team to show you all the monitoring and documentation they have for the device.

Teams

Server support and engineering teams require a higher degree of specialization than the help desk or desktop teams. You could have server engineers for e-mail, databases, applications, and operating systems. When you are building a server team, look for a balance of skills between specializations, support, and engineering personalities that work well together. Remember to build redundancy into the team so the company has support and you do not need to call someone sick or on vacation.

Hiring

The first thing to consider when hiring for server roles is what operating system and software you are using. If you are running Linux servers, the Redhat RHCE is a well-known and respected certification. The exam is a test of configuring live servers. A certified RHCE should have a good level of skill. If you have Microsoft servers, there are a number of written Microsoft tests. While these are not as accurate an indicator of real-world skills, these certifications do show initiative and ability. However, an individual's credentials should not be the only measure of the value they can bring to the company. Plenty of good technical professionals are not certified. Ask candidates about naming conventions, documentation, and ticketing systems to make sure they will work well in a structured environment.

Tactical Challenges

The tactical challenges for server teams are monitoring, major upgrades, documentation, and disaster recovery. Monitoring requires software to support all of the basic and business-critical functions. The server team should work with the help desk team for monitoring. The help desk team actively monitors the servers, and the server team usually gets e-mails or text messages when there is an issue. Major upgrades can create logistical problems. If your company has formal project managers, you should be able to turn to them for help in organizing and managing the project. If you do not, I provide tips and tricks in the project management chapter that should help.

Documentation and backups are critical issues in any group, they are also very important for network engineering in the next chapter. Technical teams rarely take the time to document and back up information. If it does happen at all, documents and backups are usually out of date and untested. A good quick test of your server team's backup strategy is to delete a file, wait a week, and ask them to recover it. If the server team cannot recovery your file, you know you need to address your backup procedures. This can be a serious issue if customer data is lost or if you are in violation of government or industry standards and regulations. Information Technology should be aware of any technology related industry or government regulations and follow them. You can find out which ones apply by speaking with the business unit, information security or audit team. Disaster recovery heavily relates to both of these topics. What is the company's plan if its servers are unavailable? Where would employees go if the office were inaccessible? All information technology teams should participate in the disaster recovery plan.

Strategic Challenges

Server teams are under increasing pressure to reduce heat and increase efficiency in rack space, power consumption, and processing power. At the same time, organizations are asking server teams to provide more services, applications, and servers. The solution that meets these requirements is blade servers. Blade servers allow typically eight to sixteen blades or servers within one chassis to share a backplane, power, and network connectivity. In addition, if you pair blade servers with external shared storage and VMware virtualization; you can create an impressive number of virtual servers. However, these new technologies add a layer of complexity that requires better–trained, highly skilled staff to manage all of these components. If your server team is not using blade servers or virtualization, you should explore and compare those options. You also need to factor in hiring and or training your staff to make the transition.

Conclusions

Server support and engineering provides the services customers and employees use to access the Internet, applications, e-mail, files, and almost every other service the business uses. Information technology managers should understand the metrics and challenges of the server team. The server teams work most closely with the network engineering team and the desktop team. Server teams need to work with the help desk on issues, and the information security team needs to work on server security. The business should factor in the needs and challenges of the server team when planning business goals.

Chapter 5
NETWORKING

Introduction

Server and network teams have important similarities and differences. Like server teams, network teams should make the same effort to get in front of customers, gather and review metrics, and it makes sense to divide the team between engineering and operations roles. There is also a major difference in understanding what the groups do and what tools they use to do it. I am assuming the reader understands what servers are, but I am not going to make that assumption about network devices. I like to explain network engineering as creating the road for applications and data to ride on or the devices that allow or prevent one computer from talking to another one. You can also look at it as everything between your computer and the corporate network and Internet. Networking happens to be my favorite role in information technology and the place I have spent most of my career. Networking may or may not be responsible for several gray areas. As a result, we should understand what the devices are so we can understand where these gray areas come up.

Companies sometimes classify firewalls as networking devices and sometimes as security devices. In my opinion, it makes more sense for networking to manage firewalls and for information security to audit and approve changes. There are several reasons I think that is effective. First, security has a conflict of interest if it is responsible for auditing the network and configuring firewalls as part of the network. However, if a separate department handles auditing, this conflict of interest may not exist. Second, when networking needs to make changes they will usually involve firewall changes as well. As a result, network changes will need to be coordinated between the network and security teams. This typically requires a high degree of coordination, involves more people, and makes the process more complicated. In addition, security and network need to work together well and have a thorough understanding of each other's roles.

There are two kinds of phone systems. Legacy phone systems are phone systems that have a connection to either a plain old telephone line, or T1 voice line, composed of voice circuits and no connection to the data network. A telecommunications team or external vendor typically manages these systems. The advantage of a legacy phone system is that data network issues will not affect the phone system. I was in New York City during the 2003 blackout and the legacy phone lines were the only thing that worked. The downside is that you cannot take advantage of new features or leverage your data network to make calls. Avaya is the most well known legacy phone system vendor. Voice over IP, or VoIP phone systems, use the data network to communicate and make calls to other VoIP phones whenever possible and only use legacy lines for calls that do not have another path. The network team or a separate phone team handles these new systems. Since VOIP systems need network connectivity and power from the network, VOIP systems usually become a network responsibility.

As we saw in the last chapter, server teams are under increasing pressure to provide more resources and services more cheaply. Blade servers have started including switches in them for network connectivity. Blade servers usually have a fiber connection to a SAN or storage area network. These connections usually happen over fiber switches, which are similar to network switches. As a result, this typically pits server and network teams at odds. Server teams want to set up blades and SANs. Network teams see these devices as network devices and are concerned about the stability of the network. There is a legitimate argument to claim these components are either server or network components. The battle does not stop with departments. Vendors are fighting over the servers and networks as well. Cisco has started building blade servers, and HP has become more aggressive with its network infrastructure strategy. These issues will take years to resolve. Management should get involved to make a determination of who is responsible and what technologies the company should use based on the merits of the technology and internal resources. As a network engineer, I believe the server teams should manage the servers and the network teams should manage blade switches and fiber switches.

Tools

Several physical components to networking include WAN circuits, cabling, wireless, routers, firewalls, and switches. WAN Circuits are connections that go outside of a company or building. WAN data circuits are the cables that telecommunications companies, such as Verizon, offer to connect to the public Internet or private networks. The private networks are either between two companies or between two offices for the same company.

If you are connecting to the Internet, you will have a choice of ordering traditional WAN technologies, such as T1 or new technologies like WAN Ethernet, Verizon FIOS, and cable. New Technologies can usually deliver the same, or more bandwidth, at a significantly cheaper than T1s and T3s. The technical considerations include the bandwidth, SLA, how many IP addresses you need, and whether you need BGP.

- Bandwidth is how much data you can send at one time. You should always choose WAN technologies that give you room to increase the bandwidth without making a physical change. This usually means Ethernet, Verizon FIOS, or cable.

- SLA is the amount of uptime the vendor will provide. You should read these agreements carefully and know whom to call when problems come up.
- Public IP addresses are a requirement for your network to be reachable from the Internet. A public IP address is required for each server you want to reach from the Internet. This could be a web server, an ftp server, or some other service. The network team should be able to do a diagram and prove how many IP addresses you need. You may need two public IP subnets if you are going to use a firewall. This topic can get complicated, so make sure you clearly understand your needs before you order.
- BGP is a protocol used to provide resilience and redundancy over the Internet. If you want this level of redundancy, make sure you have a skilled team of network engineers to support it.

There are two different ways to connect private connections—external and internal. External connections are between two different companies. Internal connections are between two different locations of the same company. Each has different considerations depending on which one you install.

Companies that require fast, reliable, and secure connections can use external connections. This is common in the financial world where companies need to send sensitive financial data between each other. This can be expensive to install and support. However, there is an alternative. If both companies have an Internet connection and devices that can create a virtual private network or VPN, you can create a secure connection over the Internet without the cost of a circuit. Both companies should have documentation with executive approval explaining the approved options, costs, and technical details. This requires a high degree of coordination between businesses and network teams. If either company does not have a capable network team with documentation, then that is a definite sign that setting up connectivity will be problematic. If this is a part of your business, you should also have current business and technical contacts for support and coordinating outages. If you do not have contacts, immediately pull this information together. If the business requires 24/7/365 support, you need to make sure you can contact the partner company if problems come up. Otherwise, the connection may be down until the next business day. If you perform overnight processing, this could result in lost revenue for one or both companies.

Internal connectivity between company locations is the easiest access to setup. You should have all the information and contacts you need. Just make sure you have someone at the other end that can work with you on connectivity. You need to know how many sites you are connecting, what bandwidth you need, and whether you need to provide Internet and from where. The best solution for small companies with only a few sites is typically to get Internet at each site and create a VPN. Middle to large size business should consider MPLS. MPLS has many benefits over traditional technologies like frame-relay and internet VPNs. Speak to your network engineering team to weigh your options, as the choice varies greatly based on your business needs.

Physical Cabling Versus Wireless

Network Engineering projects usually involve cabling or wired network, at least for the near term. Some network engineers can perform cabling work, but the vast majority of the time it makes sense to hire an outside vendor. When you hire a cabling vendor, you should look for several things. First, hire a dedicated cabling vendor. If cabling is not the main goal of the business, you should look elsewhere. I have walked into situations where companies hired a vendor with diverse services to save money and they usually needed to replace the cabling. Second, obtain an itemized quote that includes parts and labor. If the quote is not itemized, I look for another vendor. I want to know exactly what I am paying for. This applies to any vendor I hire. Third, find out if the vendor can meet your time frame. If there is a lead on materials that goes beyond a few weeks, find someone else. The vendor that cannot manage resources is not someone you want working for you. Fourth, what is the attitude of the company representatives? Are they easy to work with? Do you get along with them? Fifth, look at the numbering scheme the vendor recommends. Does it make sense? Is it easy to follow? You will be living with the cabling for a long time. If the cabling scheme does not make sense, it will create problems in the future particularly for the desktop and network engineering teams. They will need to locate where all the cable connects to support end users.

Wireless can be an alternative, but also a security risk. Anyone within range can access a wireless network without the proper security controls. WEP wireless security can be hacked in minutes. There are more secure alternatives like WPA2, but I hope this shows you some of the risk. What would happen to your business if someone had access to all your private sensitive information? If you are going to use a wireless network to conduct company business, make sure you understand the risks. Eventually, corporate networks will all become wireless when speed, security, and cost issues are addressed. You should also keep these risks in mind for your personal wireless networks. Anywhere in the United States, you can typically find a few unsecured networks. It is stealing to access these networks and you do not know who else is using them so you should avoid them at all costs.

Routers

Routers are computers dedicated to deciding which way to send data and then sending it. They typically do this through a routing protocol. If you have a network of more than a few network devices, you should be using a routing protocol. Routing Protocols are responsible for sending data from point A to point B over the most efficient, loop-free route. The most efficient route considers the number of devices the data needs to pass through, bandwidth, reliability and possibly other factors. A routing loop is when device A sends data to device B, and device B sends it back to device A, and the data never reaches its destination. All routing protocols have mechanisms to protect against this scenario. Some examples of routing protocols are RIP, EIGRP, OSPF, and BGP. Cisco is the most well known vendor, but other companies, such as Juniper, make routers as well. There is an old saying that no one ever was ever fired for buying Cisco. However, this does not mean you should not consider alternatives and do competitive pricing! Although I have never bought from Juniper, their sales presentations have impressed me.

Switches

Switches are devices that allow large numbers of phones, desktops, laptops, and servers to connect and talk to each other. The switch may also be able to perform routing like a router. Switches range from small devices that take 1U of rack space to chassis-based switches that can take half a rack and have hundreds of ports. Switches also have their own protocol to maintain a loop-free path called spanning tree protocol or STP. Cisco is the most well known vendor and, for the most part, considered the de facto standard for switching. I have tried switches from other vendors, but I have not found switches from any other vendor that I like better. As a point of full disclosure, the majority of my career has been working with Cisco products, and the majority of that has been working on switches.

Firewalls

While routers try to get traffic where it is going, firewalls try to block unwanted traffic. Firewalls are also typically the place that virtual private networks or VPNs are setup. Sometimes routers or dedicated devices will manage VPN connections. It usually makes sense to put VPNs on the firewall. Virtual private networks allow two firewalls to have a private conversation over the Internet. In order to setup a VPN, the firewall needs to have a public IP address.

There is much more variety in the firewall marketplace than either routers or switches. However, Cisco makes Cisco ASA firewalls. Some competitors are Checkpoint, Juniper, and Fortinet. If you choose to get Cisco routers and switches but use another vendor for firewalls, you may have compatibility and support issues. I prefer Cisco ASA firewalls.

Teams

Company size typically determines how to divide network teams. In a small company, the network engineer could also be responsible for the servers or other aspects of the company. A large company typically divides the network team into an operations team and an engineering team. The operations team is responsible for troubleshooting issues that come up in day-to-day operations and implements some or all network changes. The engineering team is responsible for the design, long-term network vision, and handling issues that the operations team is unable to solve. This design seems to work very well. Engineers typically fall into one of two mindsets just like server administrators. People who are good in operational roles have a sense of urgency and like excitement. People who are a good fit for engineering are more interested in planning and preparing tasks in advance. There is some variety in network engineer skill sets, but most teams will have engineers that can work on routers, firewalls, and switches.

Hiring

Network engineers need familiarity with the router and switch devices your company is managing. If the network team is managing the phone system and firewalls, they will need those skills as well. I also highly recommend at least two people on the team familiar with monitoring and some form of log in authentication like RADIUS or ACS. Network teams are generally monolithic. You want at least two engineers to manage the network in case someone is out.

Tactical Challenges

The common tactical problems are backups, documentation, monitoring, and good network design practices.

As we have seen with each of the groups so far, technical people usually work hard, but have a dislike for documentation and maintaining backups. This usually leads to poor documentation. The risk of not having backups and documentation can be catastrophic. If a router crashes and you do not have a copy of the configuration, the outage can extend significantly. These are only a couple of the problems related to documentation and backups. I explain to network engineers that it is in their benefit to have documentation and backups.

Every network engineering team should have the following documentation.

1.) Network diagram—The networking team should be able to provide current diagrams of the network. If the network team does not have current diagrams, this is a network engineering and security issue.

2.) Support contracts—The network team should have current documented support for every production device in the network infrastructure.

3.) WAN circuit information—The network team should have each WAN circuit ID labeled on the device, in the device configuration, and available to the help desk. In addition, they should provide a number to call for support. When a circuit goes down, you do not want to be looking for the circuit ID or the support number. This information should be available to the help desk and everyone in network engineering. I like to put the circuit ID and number to call on network diagrams. If you are troubleshooting a problem, you can see the design and the circuit information at the same time.

4.) Backups—The network team should be able to produce backups of all production configurations and be able to roll back when they experience issues. RANCID is a free system and Solarwinds is a commercial product that has tools to maintain backups.

5.) Templates—The network team should be able to provide templates for common configurations of devices. This makes things fast, secure, and consistent.

6.) Unified logins—All network device logins should authenticate to an authentication server like RADIUS or TACACS+. My favorite is Cisco ACS, which can tie into a Microsoft Windows domain. When someone leaves, you simply delete the windows account, which removes the network access.

Monitoring is as critical for network engineering as it is for server teams. Usually networking takes the blame for outages when no one can find another root cause because it is the least understood area of information technology. I have been able to provide monitoring charts on several occasions proving problems were not network related. While the network team will be interested in CPU, memory, and disk space, network engineering is far more concerned with the network bandwidth available, port errors, and Internet links.

Network engineering merely needs to modify the alerts server teams use, and make sure they and the help desk receive alerts if routers, switches, firewalls, circuits, or VPNs go down. Networking and Server teams should have a rotating on call schedule to take these calls after hours. Here is a sample call rotation. Each department should send a on call schedule to the help desk.

Week	Team Member	Cell	Manager/Escalation	Cell
5/2/12 - 5/8/12	Employee A	XXX-XXX-XXXX	Tom Monte	XXX-XXX-XXXX
5/9/12 - 5/15/12	Employee B	XXX-XXX-XXXX	Tom Monte	XXX-XXX-XXXX

Network design often takes a backseat to keeping the network running and projects the business units put a priority on. The effort in developing and maintaining a good network design will pay for itself many times over, because the company will not have to constantly make technical changes to support the business needs. How do you know if you have a good design? You can tell your company has a good design when you ask network engineering where to put several new devices, and they do not have to think about it or make significant changes. If you cannot do that, it is time to start a new project and redesign the network.

Strategic Challenges
Network engineering is facing an identity crisis. The lines of the network have blurred between voice, security, and servers. This is not only an issue every company faces, but also an industry wide concern. Companies should clearly define the role of the network team. I do not think there is a single solution to the problem and it is highly dependent on the history, quality of the teams involved, purchasing decisions, and much more. While this is an important concern for network engineering, management should define the roles and responsibilities of each team.

Conclusions

Network engineering is critical to a successful business and typically operates in a supporting role for other areas of information technology. Network engineering works most closely with server support and engineering to roll out new services and provide the groundwork for server communication. Network engineering also needs to work closely with information security because network vulnerabilities can lead to business risk. A good network engineering team will securely provide the tools to deploy servers and services quickly and provide users access to the Internet and partner content. The less interaction the company has with networking outside of proactive activities, the better your team is.

Network engineering, like server engineering, has little organic exposure to business units, customers, desktop support, and the help desk. This isolation can make it difficult for a network engineering team to understand the needs of the business and provide value. Make every effort to build those relationships and contribute to the success of the company.

Chapter 6
DEVELOPMENT

Introduction

I have worked in every area of information technology, except development. The closest I have come is being responsible for release deployment teams, working closely with development teams, and writing a few small programs of my own in Perl and Python. My biggest programming achievement was writing snmpping. pl. Snmpping.pl is a Perl program that tests whether a device would respond to an SNMP string. A SNMP string is like a username to send data back to a network monitoring system. The program was included in the popular MRTG program. I am particularly proud of that. Despite my lack of experience, I can still provide some useful insights about development teams from the outside.

Tools

Fast Company-Owned Desktops

The most important thing information technology can give to developers is a fast computer. All groups can benefit from a fast computer, but developers will gain a great deal of productivity from having a fast computer. Almost every program language requires compiling. Compiling a computer program is telling the computer to change the program from words people understand to programs that computers understand. The process is CPU and memory intensive, and a developer may need to repeat the process several times throughout the day. I believe slow computers have three impacts on user productivity in general. First, the user is unable to work when a system is slow or crashes and needs to take time to recover. Second, when a user expects to wait for the computer, he or she typically gets a cup of coffee, takes a bathroom break, or chats with coworkers. Typically, this takes longer than the computer does to finish a task. This creates a loss of productivity. Third, a slow computer can sap morale for a development team. I have never seen a developer turn down a fast computer, and I have made plenty of friends by championing fast machines for development. I always recommend desktops for developers. While desktops have a slight edge in power, it is not enough to justify the loss of mobility.

Why do I recommend desktops then? It has to do with intellectual property, the temptation to reach beyond development, and avoiding burnout. It is very difficult to take a desktop home with you. Employees should develop programs in the company's office to protect the intellectual property. A laptop can be stolen, it can have information removed from it onsite, and it can be connected to an uncontrolled insecure network. When you keep the computer at the office, you avoid all of those risks. However, you also need to consider where developers store and send data. Some developers will also get involved in areas outside of development, such as managing the infrastructure or working on production issues. When they have to be at the office to work, it is much more difficult to ask them to get involved in other areas, where their time will be less productive. The last issue is that developers can get passionate about a project and devote large amounts of time to it. While this may be good for the company in the short term, it is in no one's best interest in the end. The need to come to the office will also reduce the urge to spend massive numbers of hours on a project.

Integrated Development Environment

Almost every developer works in an integrated development environment or IDE. An IDE provides the developer with a place to write code, check syntax, and compile code all in one place. The system should support the language and features the developer needs, and everyone on the team should use the same tools.

Revision Control System

You need a revision control system to track the changes to professional development work. The system should be able to track changes and roll back to previous versions. Test these mechanisms on a regular basis.

Secure Offsite Backups

You may be required to maintain a copy of your software as a part of a deal with lenders, with the government, or per industry regulation. Even if you are not required to keep copies of your code, you should have a current offsite backup and at least two people who know how to install the software. This prevents any lose of continuity if a single employee leaves. If you only have two people capable of installing the software and one of them leaves, you should train someone else to maintain your redundancy.

Documentation

Document code and develop models to show how different parts of the system work together. Keep documentation up to date. A good test is to ask a random developer to explain the model and then ask another developer the same question. If the stories are the same, you probably have a team with a strategic programming vision. If they have different ideas, call a meeting and develop a strategic vision that all developers agree to that meets the business objectives. Everyone should understand the strategic goals of the team from the testers to software architects.

Teams

Developers are the core of a development team that programs applications. Build redundancy into these positions with more than one developer who understands the big picture about how the programs work.

Database developers are usually a part of the development team. They may require separate database tools to manage the databases they maintain depending on your database.

Application testers test the code that developers create to make sure it is stable and works as expected.

Release manager may be a dedicated position or a roll filled by someone in the team. The release manager coordinates the code and makes sure the entire package is ready for release.

Hiring

Developers need to be experts in the language you are developing in and know the tools you are using. Developers should have a team attitude and be willing to rotate the pieces of code they work on to create redundancy. One of the most effective interview techniques I have seen with developers is to ask the developer to build a simple prototype program. I like this model, because you get a real insight into the developers ability and style.

Tactical Challenges

If programming language is on version 10 and you are still programming on version 2, you have a problem. You are missing all the advances and bug fixes in the language. Why reinvent the wheel? This also applies to the IDE, database, development platform, and all other tools. The further you fall behind, the harder problems become, and the harder it is to find developers. If you are developing in COBOL or DOS, you definitely have a problem. Fortunately, there is a cheap way to bring developers up to speed, if at least one developer is fluent in a process or language.

You can pay for training, develop a mentoring program, or host a lunch where each developer takes a turn to talk about a topic. Lunch and learn sessions work just as well for other teams. The company should pay lunch to encourage the process. If you do pay for lunch, make sure there is plenty for everyone. A company I worked at once bought lunch and they had to cut slices of pizza in half for everyone to get a slice. This was about ten years ago and I am still annoyed about it. If you are going to buy lunch, do not be cheap about it. Lunch and learn meetings are cheap, effective ways to train your team.

Strategic Challenges

The biggest challenge for a business when working with developers is maintaining company control of the code they create. I have seen several companies at the mercy of their own developers because one or two people were the only ones who understood and could maintain business-critical code. Businesses should invest in developer redundancy, rotate which parts of the code individual developers work on, develop good documentation standards, and maintain backups of the code. This prevents a small group of developers from holding the company hostage.

Conclusions

Development allows a company to develop software that gives the company a competitive advantage. It is important that the business understands the value of its intellectual property and protects it. Developers have even less interaction with other parts of the company than server and network teams do, and it is even more critical that they reach out and understand how users use the products they develop. Of all the areas of information technology, development has the most developed models for managing its department, workflow, and user interaction. Companies will see amazing benefits from taking advantage of the wealth of development methodologies and tools.

Chapter 7
INFORMATION SECURITY
AND AUDITING

Introduction

I have read books, such as *The Cuckoo's Egg: Tracking a Spy Through the Maze of Computer Espionage* by Clifford Stoll and *Secrets of a Super Hacker* by Knightmare that made information security seem sensational and exciting. When I switched from network engineering to information security, I wanted to catch hackers and spies to save the company. The reality of information security and auditing is quite different. Information security and audit teams rely more heavily on documentation than any other part of information technology. You can actually decide whether you would like to pursue either field based on how you feel about paperwork.

Information security and auditing are very different from the other areas of IT. Information security is concerned with mitigating business risk. Audit is concerned with making sure that the company policies and procedures comply with—and that all employees follow—all government, business, and industry regulations. These groups can be one department or two separate departments. I think two separate departments make the most sense because audit should review information security procedures and policies, and information security should audit the business and technical risks from the audit team. In addition, both groups should report directly to the CEO and or CIO. If they do not, they should be providing updates directly. This eliminates risk of anyone in the chain of command filtering information from executive management. I discuss the groups together, as there is some overlap in the purpose and tools used by both teams. Both teams review and work with other teams to develop documentation and make sure employees follow it in practice.

Information security focuses on making sure that technical and process controls create an acceptable level of risk. An acceptable level of risk is whatever risks the company is comfortable with. In order to understand the level of risk, information security needs to gather information, assess risk, and make recommendations to management. In order for the process to work, all employees must participate and be involved with information security. Information security should actively engage in understanding how every department functions and what risks that presents to the business. In order to be effective, information security must develop good relationships across the entire company and with internal and external auditors.

Audit uses government regulation, industry standards, and company policies to make sure information technology departments follow company policies. Departments usually receive an audit yearly. If a company works in the financial sector or healthcare, it can be more frequent. If you process credit cards, you are obligated to follow PCI regulations. If you deal with healthcare, you need to follow HIPAA regulations. Even companies that are not in healthcare need to understand and follow HIPAA, if they have employee healthcare plans and track any kind of employee healthcare information. If an employee speaks to a manager, I discourage them from talking about specifics of medical conditions and encourage them to speak with human resources.

I think most people envision the IRS coming to collect back taxes when they think of information technology audits. Most departments try to get audits over with as quickly as possible. However, there is another way to look at an audit. If you are aware of a business risk or process that your company has not documented or followed, the audit is your chance to bring up the issue to make sure it gets attention it deserves. Even if your company does not address the issue, you have a written record that you brought the issue up.

What do you do if the audit findings say you need to fix the problem? If the concerns are valid, communicate that you will make the change, and follow up when it is done. If the concerns are not valid in your opinion, you and your management determine whether to change and issue a response to the audit explaining why not if the change will not be made. An audit is a negotiation and the findings are typically not set in stone unless the problem is a serious issue. Audits gradually become more and more detail oriented over time as you fix more and more issues. When auditors start nit picking, think of it as a sign that you and your team are doing a good job.

Tools

Documentation

Information security teams rely on a guiding set of policies to protect the company and inform customers and users about what the company expects of them. Your company should have at a minimum a security policy and an acceptable use policy. In addition, it is a good idea to require yearly security training for all employees. The security policy describes the entire security program. The acceptable use policy describes what users may do, and every user should sign the agreement stating they will follow all security policies. The SANS institute is a research organization of individuals from around the world. You can get templates for your company's policies from them at http://www.sans.org/security-resources/policies/. Audit relies primarily on documentation from other teams and sometimes asks to see output proving the findings presented. Information security uses the rest of the tools.

Intrusion Detection System (IDS) / Intrusion Prevention System (IPS)

Information security teams have a tool to detect and stop attacks on the network. Intrusion Detection systems and intrusion prevention systems are servers or appliances that are placed at the edge of the network near Internet connectivity. They capture and analyze data passing through the network and compare them against signatures. Signatures are criteria the IDS or IPS match against such as a particular port, protocol, IP address, or URL. Once data matches a signature, this is where the IDS and IPS differ. The IDS can only alert information technology about threats. The IPS is able to stop the data by sending a command back to the source to stop sending. When you are setting up an IPS, place it in an IDS or watching mode until you are sure you know how the device will act with your data. It is very easy to cause a mistake that will disrupt the business.

SEIM

Information security teams can use a SEIM to gather logs from servers, desktops, and network devices and aggregate all the data to determine if there is an attack on the network. These devices can be very helpful in getting a picture of how your network interacts between desktops, servers, and network infrastructure.

Firewalls

I discussed firewalls in the chapter on networking, but the same ideas apply if an information security team manages them.

Two Factor Authentication Systems

Authentication is an important part of making sure the right people have access to company systems. It also keeps the wrong people out. There are three ways to determine that the right people have access. Something a person is, like a finger print for a biometric scan. Something a person has, like a gift card. Something someone knows, like a password. You have two factor authentication when you require a person to have two of these forms of validation. The most common form of two-factor authentication is a physical key with a code that changes at regular intervals and a pass code. The most well known two factor key is an RSA SecurID key. If someone gets hold of the physical key or the password, that person will be unable to access the system. Two factor provides a much higher level of security for access. Every company should consider making this investment.

Security Advisories

Information security teams should subscribe to, and regularly watch for, security threats and updates. Here are a few places you should look for those updates. Security teams should have a list of vendors for the technologies the company owns. The information security team should keep an eye on each vendor's security advisory page for flaws and security issues. In addition, every information technology team should track security advisories for the devices they manage. Security is everyone's responsibility and this approach provides two levels of security. Security does not stop at advisories. Everyone involved should be checking and following best industry practices for all devices. In addition, US CERT is a government site dedicated to security that you can find at http://www.us-cert.gov/ .

Teams

Information security and audit teams require specialized skills like server and network teams. Look at all the technologies that your company relies on and make sure you hire information security professionals with those skills. You also need to keep in mind that your team needs redundancy in the skills the team has. Since information security needs to monitor all aspects of information technology, this can be a difficult balancing act. You may need to rely on internal cross training to get the desired level of redundancy. If you are in an industry with little need for oversight or technology services, you may not need much in the way of an information security team. However, if you are a bank or government institution, you will need a strong security program.

Hiring

Information security professionals have a number of certifications. The most well-known and vendor agnostic certification is the CISSP. In the interest of full disclosure, I am a certified CISSP. I think the CISSP teaches the basic principles of information security and is a good indicator that an individual is serious about information security as a profession. The most popular audit certification is the CISA. However, you should not hire solely based on any credential. Information security professionals should be very detail oriented, good at paperwork, and process focused. They should also have good interpersonal skills because they will need to build relationships across the company to be effective.

Tactical Challenges

Information security and audit teams need to avoid losing sight of the big picture. I have seen many productive relationships between information security and other parts of information technology sour because of information security policies. Information security should understand how security decisions affect the rest of information technology. An information security team that asks the desktop team to manually edit 10,000 laptops will not make many friends. If the exploit is theoretical, the company won't be much more secure either. Information security breaches usually occur either from someone inside the company or an obvious flaw. The mission-impossible style attacks are highly unlikely and unnecessary if you neglect to lock the proverbial front door. It is far more productive to close the accounts of employees that leave a company, turn off unnecessary services, turn on encryption, and tighten a firewall than it is to close obscure theoretical vulnerabilities. If you have taken care of documentation and basic issues, you should definitely tackle more obscure and unlikely attacks. Every company I have ever worked for has a few obvious problems. You should focus on those first.

Strategic Challenges

Information security and audit teams have the same strategic risks. Every company has technology risks and they will be different for every company based on technology, people, and business models. The only completely secure company is the ones that are no longer doing business. The art of information security and auditing is to understand the balance between security and keeping the business operating effectively. Validate all decisions against not what is most secure, but by a reasonable level of risk that allows the company to make a profit.

Conclusions

The information security and audit teams are the watchdogs of the company. The purpose of these teams is to manage the risk the company faces. Companies should view these groups not as an imposition imposed on the business by government and industries, but as partners in managing risk and keeping the company profitable. A smart business will calculate and put a price on what a security breach would cost the company in terms of revenue and reputation. This is the same risk analysis we saw with anti-virus software. After completing this exercise, I guarantee that you will not look at your information security and audit departments as cost centers again.

Chapter 8
PROJECT MANAGEMENT

Introduction

Project management is a unique department in many ways. Project management is a skill that all departments practice whether they are aware of it or not. In many ways, it bridges the gap between customers, partners, information technology teams, and management to accomplish project objectives. I have practiced project management out of necessity over many years of working in information technology on large projects. As a result, I have developed my own ideas and methodologies around project management. The most successful project I ever had was a business critical, load-balancer replacement. I had over a month to prepare, and when the day came to make the change, we followed every line on the project plan, and the project was successful. The ability to execute a plan exactly the way the project manager wrote it, line by line, is my standard for a well-executed project.

However, I realized that my own discoveries were not good enough, and I decided to pursue a formal certification with the PMP. I passed in 2009. The Project Management Institute offers a PMP certification, and it is widely respected. I discovered that many of the ideas I developed were already best practices. I highly recommend that all information technology professional get PMP certified to get a strong understanding of project management.

Keys to successful project management:

- Scope—Define at the very beginning of the project what you are going to deliver. Almost every project I have worked on started with a vague verbal definition of the goals of the project. It is impossible to succeed, without agreement on what you are going to do. The scope is a formal document that states the goals of the project. It is important that everyone involves agrees to the goals stated in the scope.
- Resources—You need to have a budget, employee time, and a timeline established at the same time as the scope. You also need to be clear that if the resources or scope changes, the delivery date will also change.
- Schedule—There should be a clear written plan of the steps involved in completing the project, and all people on the team should understand the deliverables and who is delivering them. Share the written project with everyone involved in the project no matter how big or small a role the person plays.

- Checkpoints—The project team should meet regularly to discuss the status of the project and any risks. I like to have weekly meetings in the late morning or early afternoon. Once the team identifies a risk, someone should be assigned to remediate the issues and report back to the team. Celebrate milestones in the project. These celebrations are good for morale and make people feel appreciated.
- Attention to detail—The more attention you pay to detail the more successful you will be. Obviously, there are practical limits, but most people, in my opinion, do not pay enough attention to details.

Tools
Project Management Software
The most well known, project management software is Microsoft Project. However, there are other alternatives, and Microsoft Project may be overkill for the scope of a project. When I have had to perform very small projects, such as a single maintenance window with a few steps, I have used e-mail or excel. I always use Microsoft Project to track larger-scale projects. Develop a template so you execute every project the same way and miss nothing. I always put a version number on every project plan I create. Project plans change frequently and it can get confusing very quickly, if you do not track the changes.
Spreadsheets
I love spreadsheets. If I get a list of items, I immediately dump them in a spreadsheet and sort them. Although spreadsheets are not strictly necessary, I have a hard time remembering any project where I did not need a spreadsheet to track something.
Business Policies and Procedures
Project managers need to be familiar with company procedures and policies related to projects. They may also need to be familiar with any client policies and procedures.

Teams
Project Management teams are composed of project managers that each handle a set of projects for the company. Project managers usually work independently within the project management team and spend most of the time coordinating with other teams and clients.
Hiring
Project managers need a good understanding of project management, interpersonal skills, and should be subject matter experts. I have managed many technology projects and it has been extremely useful to understand the technology the team is trying to implement. I am completely helpless around the house. I would not be the best choice for project manager on a construction project. Yet, many project managers work on projects where they are not familiar with the subject matter. I do not think this is a good fit and if you find yourself in this situation,

you should learn about the subject of the project. Interpersonal skills are also important because project managers frequently need to interact with and coordinate large groups of people from different departments.

Tactical Challenges

Project managers need to have good relationships within the company and possibly with clients in other companies. A project manager that has poor relationships will ultimately be unable to drive the project to success. Project managers also need to track issues, make sure goals are reasonable, smooth out issues between stakeholders, and escalate identified risks. They also need to take into consideration the opinions and suggestions of people involved in the project. A project manager who dictates dates without making sure they are reasonable is frustrating to work with and usually ends up missing deadlines.

Strategic Challenges

Companies and information technology departments rarely take advantage of project management. When a project does not have a dedicated project manager, performance and success usually suffer. Even if project manager resources are scarce, it is well worth the effort to spend some time getting project manager input on a project.

Conclusions

Project management should be an integral part of any project. Project managers are critical resources to delivering projects successfully. Project managers are the glue that holds everything together to complete a project on budget and on time. They fill the gaps between departments, customers, and management.

Chapter 9
HIRING

I usually review one hundred resumes on average to get four candidates for a phone screen and then usually average two in-person interviews to fill one position. This means your chances of getting a job from me are one in one hundred. A rough estimate of my time is five minutes per resume, an hour per phone screen, two hours per in-person interview, and five hours consulting with human resources. This comes out to about twenty-two hours for every position. When you consider how busy most managers are, this is a tremendous time investment. Why do I devote so much time to hiring?

Most companies would benefit from attaching more importance to hiring. When you think about it, hiring decisions are the most important decisions any company ever makes. It is equally important to a perspective employee; your financial future depends on getting a job. Ironically, when you are the hiring manager, the same is true. If you hire the wrong person, it could end up causing you grief for years to come or, worse, get you fired. If you have never hired someone before, this chapter gives you a good idea about how the process works. If you have hired people before, you will pick up some new tricks when you recruit for your next open position.

Human resources can be an invaluable partner in helping you through the hiring process. Keep human resources updated on the status of open positions all the way through the process. Some managers refuse to include human resources because they are concerned human resources will interfere or delay a decision. Based on my experience, I have always worked with human resources and never had any problems.

I present each step in the process from the point of view of a perspective employer and perspective employee. This provides both groups with valuable insights into how the process works and what each side of the process.

Obtaining Permission to Hire

Companies hire employees when someone leaves or the business expands. When the business expands, sometimes it is hard to convince management that you need more employees. The best way to convince management you need to hire someone is to track the number of hours your team works and what he or she are working on. Here is a simple example of time management for a team. Use this sample chart to convince management that it is time to hire another person. The chart clearly shows that Employee A needs more help in server administration.

Routine Hours Updated							
Person	Position	Management	Meetings	Support	Projects	Monitoring	Total
Thomas Monte	Manager	10	15	5	20	0	50
Employee A	Server	0	2	20	30	25	77
Employee B	Network	0	2	30	5	0	37
Employee C	Help Desk	0	5	20	5	10	40
Totals		10	24	75	60	35	204

If I were the manager you are trying to convince, I would want to get a better understanding of how you arrived at those numbers. Be prepared to back up your chart with evidence to support the numbers. Hiring has a cost beyond the salary of an employee, as benefits, training, and taxes are a significant expense to the company. If your manager approves your request to hire another employee, he may need to cut budget somewhere else, so remember to be appreciative. Once you have convinced your manager that it is time to hire, pull information together to share with human resources.

Job Descriptions and Salaries

Every job search should start with a job description and every employee should have a job description. Job descriptions are a useful tool. They immediately tell anyone you are working with exactly what you are looking for. It also tells employees what you expect. Human resources usually provide a template for job descriptions. If they do not, you need at least the following information: title, department, reporting structure, job summary, job description, and job requirements. I put these four things in every job description I write.

1.) Complete other duties as assigned. If employees read job descriptions literally, they can say you are asking them to do things beyond the scope of their jobs. This catchall allows you to assign duties that are not explicitly stated.

2.) You must be able to lift fifty pounds. I always put this in job descriptions because information technology professionals order heavy servers and switches and need to install them. You cannot discriminate based on gender, disability, or appearances, but you can state that you require lifting.

3.) You must have a valid driver's license. Information technology employees may need to drive to other locations or a data center. I always put this requirement into job descriptions.

4.) You must be legally allowed to work in the United States. It is illegal to ask if a candidate has a green card. All candidates need to prove they are allowed to work in the United States on the first day on an I9 form.

Once you have a job description, you need to settle on a salary. You may not have much leeway on this, or it may be totally up to you. The best way to get an idea of the going rate is to check salaries online, or look at the pay for similar jobs at online job sites. You should never publish what you are willing to pay for a position.

This will hurt your ability to negotiate later, but you can share a range with human resources and any recruiters you work with. The best way to get a range is to take the maximum you are willing to pay and subtract 10 percent. The best candidate is not always the one that wants the most money. Once you think you have a reasonable salary, you are ready to speak with human resources.

Job candidates should read job descriptions carefully and make sure they qualify for the position. Some job descriptions are vague and some are specific. If I see a job where I have 80 percent of the qualifications, a reasonable commute, and the job looks interesting, I apply. The worst that can happen is I will not get a response.

Finding Job Candidates

You can search for the candidate yourself or get help in your search. The decision of which path to take will probably be decided for you based on company policy and resources.

Most companies have a policy that you must first post all jobs internally. This method is free, references are available by speaking with coworkers, and you will be able to skip many steps in the employment process. It is also good for company morale. Employees will see that it is possible to achieve promotion without having to leave the company. Despite these benefits, there are some internal political risks in dealing with the employee and his current manager. If others in the company perceive you as poaching members of other teams, you will lose trust with other managers. If you turn down qualified employees, others will perceive you as violating company policy. If you talk to the manager and/or employee, you run the risk of getting in the middle of whatever caused the employee to look in the first place.

I have a simple solution to all of these awkward situations. Whenever an employee from another department approaches me about a job on my team, I tell them to ask their manager and confirm that it is ok. This completely removes me from the situation. If the other manager does agree to allow the employee to move, I stay flexible about the transition. I usually agree to the employee moving to my team in two or three weeks, but ask them to be available for up to a month to assist their old team. Other managers will usually be grateful for the additional time. After all, they would have only gotten two weeks if the employee quit. Personally, I have a policy of never stopping anyone who wants to move into another position. If you stop them from leaving the team, they will leave the company. If you let them move, you have someone you know well in another team.

While you pursue candidates internally, you should also look externally. Human resources may want to find candidates for you using their own tools. I set up a meeting with human resources and discuss what I am looking for. I bring the price range and job description that I developed when I started the process. In addition, I ask for good interpersonal skills and one or two technical skills at a high level. These could be certifications like PMP or CISSP, but I usually like to stick to job titles, such as network engineer. This keeps the search simple for human resources and does not require them to be technical experts. I have not had much luck with this method, but it does not take much effort, and you should follow the policy set by human resources. Whenever human resources send me a candidate, I write back with feedback on why I want to interview the candidate or not. This lets human resources know that I am an active partner in the process and helps them narrow the scope. If I do interview a candidate, I send that feedback as well. If I really need to fill a role and human resources has not been able to provide a good candidate, I suggest that we look at alternative methods. However, if I need to find a replacement immediately, I politely suggest that we pursue multiple options at the same time.

You can perform the search yourself by asking people you know, checking your personal professional networks, or checking job-board websites. If you know someone directly or indirectly, you will be able to get good references, help a friend, and fill the position without a significant cost to the company. If you are a member of a professional organization like PMI for project managers, you might be able to find someone through them. Your company may also have access to a job board like www.dice.com or www.monster.com.

The last way to find candidates is through headhunters or recruiting agencies, who are professionals that find employees to fill positions. This is the most effective and controversial. Human resources will usually have an approved list. If they do not, or you have someone you would like to use, you should meet with human resources and see if you can get your agency approved. Make sure you are working with an ethical, respected partner. Most information technology professionals have a story about a bad experience, but I have also worked with some excellent headhunters that helped my career, too. Here are some of the things I like to watch out for.

- Poaching is the process of placing new employees at a company and using those contacts to find employees they can entice to leave. When the employee or employees leave, they can fill those positions, too. I never ask the headhunter that placed me at a company to help me find my next job. It puts them in an uncomfortable ethical dilemma.
- Scattershot is when a recruiting agency takes a candidate's resume or a company position and posts it at every conceivable source and hope that something sticks. The candidate can end up submitted to the same position multiple times. When I see the same resume multiple times, I refuse to work with that agency and the candidate. Recruiters and candidates that use this approach are showing they really do not care where they work and are not interested in your company.
- Misrepresentation from recruiters is frustrating. I have seen them misrepresent a candidate's skill set. I have also been on the receiving end as a candidate. A headhunter called me with an opportunity I had already rejected. He called me back with a more interesting position with the same company. When I showed up for the interview, I found

out he scheduled me for the job I had turned down. I never worked with him again and I do not think many other people have either.

- Personal interest is very important to me. Headhunters that treat me like a meal ticket don't get my business as a candidate or an employer. I always look for headhunters that want to hear what I am interested in and get to know me. Customer service applies to all businesses.

Once you have made an agreement with human resources, let them set the fee with the recruiting agency. Human resources will always be able to get a better deal because they are subject-matter experts and can open up opportunities in other departments. In addition, if human resources and the agency argue over the fees, you are not involved, and it will not hurt your relationship with human resources or the agency. Although you should never need to negotiate fees, you should know what they are. Fees can range from 5 percent to 30 percent of a yearly salary. This can be a significant amount of money whether you are a candidate or client. As a result, I always expect good service in either role. In addition, there are many agencies, so you do not need to settle. Since you do not pay them unless they are successful, they are usually very motivated to help. If a candidate does not stay for six months, the agency will usually offer to find a replacement free, and sometimes they aren't paid. There are benefits to working with a headhunter whether you are an employer or a candidate. If you remember back at the beginning of the chapter, I spend over twenty hours per new hire. A good headhunter can quickly narrow the candidates down to four or five phone screens that can result in a hire. The amount of time saved can be worth the fees. If you are a candidate, a good headhunter will have access to jobs you don't see posted anywhere else. This can cut down your competition from the entire web to a handful of alternatives. In both capacities, it is important to your career to cultivate long-term relationships with headhunters.

When you are candidate, there are only three options. You can let your professional network know you are looking, apply on job boards, or post your resume. It makes sense to leverage all three. As a candidate, expect to apply for roughly one hundred jobs to get one offer. Many candidates do not take the time to apply to that many jobs and end up with a longer search and a less desirable job. I have also found that the more money you make, the longer a search takes. There are fewer high paying jobs and more people interested in taking them.

Resumes

The resume is an often-neglected art in the pursuit of work. People rarely take the time to cultivate a good resume. A resume is worth the entire salary of your new job, because without it you will not even get an interview. When I review resumes, I look for several things, and candidates should do several things to stand out.

	Interviewer	Candidate
Skills	When I search for resumes, I pick two or three key words to search for.	If you are a candidate, make sure you have REO™. REO is resume engine optimization. Resume optimization is making sure you have the right buzzwords on your resume, such as certifications or marketable skills that you possess.
Spelling and Grammar	While I am not fanatical about spelling and grammar, obvious mistakes show a lack of attention to detail.	You should use a word processor and double check your work.
No Gaps	If a candidate has long unexplained gaps of time on a resume, I discard it. This shows the candidate is probably unreliable.	If you are unemployed or a stay-at-home mom, you can still explain those times. I would accept seeing stay at home mom, school, or "consultant" over no explanation. Life happens, and I can accept that as an employer.
Experience	Experience is king. The more real-world experience you have, the more likely you will get an interview.	If you do not have much experience, you should focus on certifications.
Certifications	I think certifications hold value and show some experience in a field. However, I would not avoid hiring candidates if they did not have a certification. However, certifications are the lazy-manager's filter. It is easier to type a certification credential and filter candidates than look at resumes.	If you do not have certifications in your area of expertise, you should get them. If not, you will be missing many opportunities.
College Degrees	I think college degrees have a benefit, but they are not the only factor.	There are definitely many good reasons to get a college degree. You will definitely hit a ceiling in career growth if you do not have a bachelor degree. If you have a bachelor degree, you should consider a Masters or Doctorate, particularly if your employer will pay for it.

Early in my career, I switched jobs every couple of years, so my resume was always current. When I finally settled down at a company, I neglected my resume for years. When I went to look for a job, I realized that my resume was terribly out of date, and I had forgotten plenty of interesting projects and technologies. Once I updated it, I looked at it every few months and made sure I had something significant to add every year. I will be able to add author to my resume with this book! This is a unique way to set you apart from other candidates and I am thoroughly enjoying the process.

Phone Screening

The phone screen is a short phone call with a candidate before you ask him or her to come in for an in-person interview. I highly recommend taking this extra step. It will help you weed out candidates that have either misrepresented their qualifications or do not fit the role. The call can last from five minutes to an hour.

The goal of the interviewer is to filter out as many unsuitable candidates as possible. The interviewer should have the job description, the candidate's resume, and a pen to take notes. I use a pen to highlight the technical skills I want to discuss on the candidate's resume and refer back to it throughout the interview. Use a private office or a conference room to conduct your interviews so you have privacy. The phone screen also saves time. The more time you spend with a candidate you are not going to hire, the less time you spend finding the right candidate. Even if I realize in the first two minutes the candidate is not going to work out, I wait for five to ten minutes out of courtesy before ending the call. A short phone screen is a bad sign, if you are a candidate.

I always cover three topics in the phone screen: the company, the job, and the candidate's technical qualifications. The first thing I ask candidates is what they know about the company and the job. Successful candidates will have done some research and be able to describe the company and the job. If candidates do not know, I give a brief overview of the company and position. This gives candidates an idea of what to expect and how they measure against the ideal candidate. It also gives candidates a chance to get comfortable, before I start asking questions. Once I do that, I go through technical qualifications. I approach each topic the same way. My first question is how they would rate their technical skills in each area from one to ten. Ten would be an expert and one would be basic knowledge. My next question is an open-ended question about that technology. Based on candidates' answers I learn two things. First, I learn what skill level they have. Second, I learn what they think they know. It is a problem when candidates think they have a high skill level but demonstrate poor working knowledge. Open-ended questions are also a good way of interviewing for skills you do not have. If candidates can explain the skills to you, they obviously have a good grasp of the topic. You can also refer back to the technical chapters to get some background on what is important for each technical qualification.

My biggest pet peeve in interviewing is candidates that put skills on a resume they cannot perform. If you need to say, "I haven't done that in a long time" or "I built a blade server in my basement," it should not be on your resume. It is the quickest way to lose a job working for me. The candidate has just wasted the time I could have invested in a qualified candidate. I like to call these resumes, buzzword resumes. Buzzword resumes have every possible qualification and skill. Most of these candidates cannot do anything posted on the resumes.

Sometimes phone screens can take unexpected turns. I had one candidate spend the entire interview complaining about a previous boss. It made me wonder what he would say about me if I hired him. I have also had phone screens go in a positive direction when a candidate had good things to say about customer service, technology, or a shared interest.

Some subjects you should never bring up in any professional capacity. I am not a lawyer or human resources professional nor am I responsible for your actions. You should check with human resources to make sure you know every topic to avoid. Discrimination is against the law. You should never discuss race, religion, sexual orientation, disabilities, veterans, or health care issues. You may be allowed to discuss politics, but I recommend avoiding it. People can be very passionate about politics. The best way to protect yourself from any legal or company action is to take detailed notes, and focus all of your conversation on the candidate's technical qualifications. If the candidate or anyone you work with tries to steer the conversation toward one of these potentially dangerous topics, try switching the topic to the weather. It is impossible to run into a problem talking about the weather.

When you finish each phone screen, write notes with your candid assessment form. This can be a formal form from human resources or just an email. Keep a copy for yourself, one for your manager, and one for human resources. It will show your manager and human resources you are serious about finding a qualified candidate and let them know what you are looking for. In addition, this protects you from accusations and lawsuits. Candidates that try to sue you or your company will have a difficult time if you have detailed notes about conversations and reasons you did not hire them. This has never happened to me, but I have gotten positive feedback from managers and human resources on taking a few minutes to complete notes for each candidate.

If you are a candidate, you are trying to prove you deserve an in-person interview. If you refer back to the beginning of the chapter, it is easy to work out the basic probability of getting a job if you are interviewing with me. Your chances of getting the job from the phone screen are about twenty-five percent. If you get an in-person interview, you chances improve to thirty to fifty percent.

Make a good impression during phone screens, which usually occur during business hours. The last thing you want is an interruption during the call, so I recommend sitting in your car. If you stand outside, background noise may make it difficult to hear and concentrate. I once had no other choice but to take a phone screen on the street in Manhattan. It was an unpleasant experience. I had difficulty hearing and concentrating. The interview did not go well. You should also have the job description, your resume, a pen for notes, the interviewer's name and number, and web research on the company. I always do a web search on the interviewer and the company. I want to make sure the company is financially stable and they have not been in the news recently for the wrong reasons. I also check out www.glassdoor.com to see what current employees think of the company. This can give you unique insight that you cannot get any other way. Now that you have done all the planning, the last thing to do is to wait for the call. Interviewers like to control when the calls happen, so they usually place the call.

Before you receive the call, have all your research laid out in front of you. Answer each question as directly and succinctly as possible. When they ask you about a technology you do not know, you have two options. First, you can tell the interviewer how it relates to the experience you do have. Second, if you do not know something, do not be afraid to say, "I don't know how to do that, but I am a fast learner, and I will look it up on the Internet." This shows the interviewer that you know how to figure things out, and you are not afraid to admit when you do not know something. The most dangerous people in information technology are the people that think they know everything. The most confident and skilled people are not afraid to admit they do not know something. Look for opportunities to explain to interviewers what you know about them and their companies. After the interview, write down your notes. If it did not go well, figure out what adjustments you need to make for next time. If it did go well and you are working with a headhunter, give them feedback after the interview. Always send an e-mail thanking the interviewer for the interview. Very few people take this step, but it can put candidates on top for an in-person interview.

In-Person Interviews

There are several things an interviewer should do to prepare for the in person interview. First, reserve an office or conference room for the meeting. Second, let reception know who you are expecting and where to reach you when they arrive. It will appear unprofessional to the candidate if no one can find you. Reception should have candidates fill out required human resources forms before they call you for the interview. Third, you should have any other interviewers prepared to meet the candidate.

Most managers interview the candidate by themselves and make the decision alone. Why carry the weight of the world on your shoulders when you can share the burden? I always offer to include human resources, my team, my manager, and several respected peers. When my team participates, I assess whether they have ever interviewed someone before. If they do not have interview experience, I ask them to stick to technical questions and I remind them not to ask personal questions. Most people are flattered that you care about their opinion and want them to participate, and it definitely improves your reputation within the company. In addition, other people bring different insights and technical experience that can help in making a decision. There is one more benefit to including several people in the interview process. You will not always make the best hiring decision no matter how good you are. If other people are involved in the decision, it is much harder to blame you, as the hiring manager, for the decision.

Once candidates have successfully passed the phone screens, I focus on interpersonal questions in the in-person interviews. This gives me a chance to read body language and see how comfortable they are dealing with other people. As we saw with the technical sections, interpersonal skills are important and frequently neglected. Keep in mind that everyone gets a little nervous in interviews and avoid being too harsh in your critique. One of my favorite and most revealing questions is, "Describe a situation where you had an interpersonal conflict with another employee or customer and how you resolved it." A good answer to this question can get a candidate a job, and a bad one can take them out of the running. What I look for is a real point of disagreement and the candidate's attempt to reach a compromise with the person they disagreed with. The worst answer is saying that this has never happened to you. Anyone who tells you they never had a disagreement at work is lying. Disagreements at work happen all the time; it is how you resolve them that matters. I usually ask a few follow up questions to make sure I understand the story, and sometimes I add hypothetical changes in the story and ask how they would react. If you do not like my question, come up with one of your own. The other question I like to ask is how a candidate resolved a recent technical problem. This is a good way to get an understanding of how someone approaches technical problems. In addition, review your phone screen notes and ask any questions you want to follow up on.

When candidates leave, thank them for their time, and let them know you will be in touch with them or the headhunter that presented the candidate. When candidates take the time to come in to meet you, they deserve the courtesy of a call back letting them know whether they got the job or not. If a headhunter presented the candidate, it is much easier to let them know they didn't get the job because you give the headhunter your feedback. The headhunter takes care of the rest. I call back candidates that I am definitely not considering immediately. Any candidates that I might consider hiring, I do not call back until I receive an accepted offer. Sometimes your first choice will turn you down, and you can still go with your second choice without that candidate knowing he or she was the second choice. If I knew I was the second choice, I would not accept a job. I do not think anyone else should either.

If a company asks, you to interview in person that means you are more than likely one of two or three remaining candidates for the job. Although, sometimes a company will not chose anyone and will look for another group of candidates. When you go to the interview, remember to dress professionally and bring several copies of your resume, some pens, and spare paper. Dressing professionally means wearing a suit for men and a professional outfit for women. Try to wear solid, sub-dued colors like gray, black, and blue. This shows that you are serious and professional. I once interviewed a candidate that showed up in a black dress shirt and an American flag tie. While I appreciate patriotism, this is not appropriate attire. Show up fifteen minutes early to the interview to show that you will be punctual. If you are not familiar with the location, leave early and bring something to read. Bring your notes from the phone interview, the job description, and any research you have on the company. I usually review my notes in my car until it is fifteen minutes to the interview before I walk into the interview.

When you meet the interviewer, shake hands and follow the interviewer's instructions. Handshakes are a funny thing and actually help form my opinion of someone. A weak handshake or an overly aggressive vise-like grip is equally bad. During the interview, be open, honest, and repeat all the things you did right on the phone screen. Regardless of the position, find a way to mention that you see your job as customer service. I have never received a bad response, and almost every time it helped my chances. It also happens to be true! This book is all about providing customer service. Keep in mind that you are interviewing your prospective employer as well. I once took an interview in lower Manhattan. The job was for a top company, and it was an exciting position that I was very interested in and uniquely suited for. I went to the interview with every intention of accepting the job. However, when I turned to leave and saw the other employees, they all looked miserable. I knew from the looks on their faces that I should not accept the job, so I turned it down. However, if you are getting ready to leave and you are interested in the job, you should tell the interviewer you are excited about the job.

What you do after an interview depends on whether you are working with a headhunter, the company's human resources department, or are on your own. If you worked with a headhunter or human resources at the company you applied to, call after your interview to provide feedback. They will usually call you back in the next day at the latest to let you know where you stand. They may ask you to come back for a second interview, tell you that you did not get the job, or make an offer. If you applied directly, you just have to wait. I continue to interview until I have accepted an offer because it is not over until you have a job. Several times, I stopped interviewing because I was sure I got a job and ended up not getting it. I do not do that anymore.

Salary Negotiation

Salary negotiations can come up during an interview, after the interview, or both. If an interviewer discusses salary during the interview, you know they are seriously considering hiring you. They may also call after the interview or work through a headhunter to bring up salary. If you are working with a headhunter or human resources, refer the interviewer to them. This avoids an uncomfortable negotiation with someone you hope to end up working for. Of course, if they press you, answer the questions. If you are a candidate that applied directly for a job, how do you answer questions about salary? You will usually get one of two questions.

The most likely question is "How much are you making now?" If they ask you your current salary, be honest and answer directly. Employers are aware that some people may inflate their base salary to get a better salary at the job they are applying for. I have had to show a paystub proving my salary a few times. It was never a problem, because I do not lie about my salary. If you cannot provide one, the employer will automatically remove you from consideration. This pretty much locks in your new salary at 5 percent to 10 percent more than you are making now in base salary. I have never seen a company offer more than that for mid- to senior-level positions. If you are just starting out, it is possible to make bigger jumps in pay.

However, there is one way to get an employer to consider a bigger increase. I always mention my benefits and any other factors that make my current job more attractive. I will add something like; "I only pay $50 per month in healthcare for a family of four" if I know the new company's plan is expensive. If you do not have this information, say it will depend on the benefits package. I also mention cost of living if I think it is more than my current location. Anytime I receive an offer to work in a city like New York City or Philadelphia, I bring up the city tax that will increase my expenses. In addition, complement the prospective employer on anything else that makes the job attractive to you such as learning from experienced technical people, the location, or training programs. You want to show them that you are looking for more than just a paycheck. One of my greatest career regrets was not getting a job at a company that had a free nacho machine!

The other question that you will get is "How much are you looking to make?" This question can be easy or difficult to answer, depending on whether you know the salary range. Some job postings will post a salary the job is offering, and if they do, you know exactly what to answer. If I am making $100,000 and a job I am a credible candidate for offers $120,000, I will tell the interviewer I want to make $120,000. If I do not have that information, the question is much harder. What I usually try to do is answer the "How much are you making now?" question. If they press me on the issue, I say that I need to consider the entire package. If the interviewer insists,

I offer 10 percent above my current salary. Now I have revealed my secrets, so I will have to change things a little for future employers reading this book!

When you are the employer, first ask what a candidate is looking to make and then, how much they make. If a candidate earns $50,000 and says he wants to earn $51,000, if you were willing to pay $55,000, you saved the company $4,000. However, you also do not want to be too cheap. I want employees to come into the company thanking me for the opportunity and not cursing me for low-balling them during salary negotiations. You still want to go through this exercise because it lets you, as the employer, control the price. If a smart candidate uses my tactics, I do not press them on the issue, as I have always felt that is tacky and pushy. If I am not willing to give candidates a small adjustment in salary, they should not be at this phase to begin with. I typically give them five to ten percent more than current base depending on how well they interviewed and fit in the position.

Making the decision

I like to have at least two good in-person interviews on the same day with the same interviewers. This makes it much easier to make a decision because one candidate usually stands out. After I complete all the interviews, I meet with each interviewer individually to get feedback on the candidates so that I can make a decision. I prefer to meet with each interviewer individually to avoid anyone influencing another's opinion. When I started using this process, I was surprised at the level of consensus interviewers have on candidates. Every interviewer likes the same candidate almost every time. Sometimes, you end up with no clear candidate. When this happens, look for a new batch of candidates. You are better off starting the process over rather than hiring someone because he or she was the last person standing. If you have one great candidate, you are ready to extend an offer. If you have two excellent candidates, you have a tough decision.

To handle a difficult decision, write down the options and weigh them against each other. The chart below is an example that will help you decide. If that does not work, poll the interviewers one more time for a decision. If you are evaluating two candidates, add more detail based on the job role.

Rated 1 to 5; higher is better	Candidate A	Candidate B
Technical Skill	3	3
Customer Service	4	2
Salary Requirements	2	3
Total	9	8

If you still cannot decide, work with your interview team to get a decision. If you think, someone is a great candidate and there is another position available, try to get him or her an interview. You want to make sure they know you set it up for them.

Extending the Offer

Once you have selected the candidate for the job and a good salary to offer, you are ready to make an official offer. Go back to human resources and your manager and let them know about your decision, and confirm that you can extend the offer. Sometimes human resources will want to extend the offer and sometimes you will. If the candidate accepts, then you have hired a new employee and you should inform human resources. If human resources extend the offer, call the candidate to congratulate them and tell them you are excited to work with them. If the candidate turns down your offer and you have an alternative, extend the offer to your second choice.

If you are the candidate and you receive a job offer, make an informed decision. You need to know the salary, potential bonuses, health benefits, work location, what your commute will be, how well you liked the people you met, and what you thought of the company. Ask for documentation on the health care options and any discounts or perks the company offers. A good company will appreciate the fact that you are taking the offer seriously, so do not be shy. Also, ask the company for a night to think about it and promise to call with an answer in the morning. I always make better decisions when I get a full night's sleep. If you have a significant other, talk it over with him or her that night. Call back the next morning with your decision. You should thank the employer for the opportunity and tell them anything special that swayed your decision. Who doesn't love to be thanked and complimented?

If you accept the offer, confirm three things before you put in notice with your current employer. You do not want to end up in a position where you quit your current job and lose the new one. These steps will protect you from that happening. First, if the new company requires a background check, financial check, or drug test, you should not put in notice until all of those checks have cleared successfully. Second, you need to agree on a start date. The industry standard is to provide your current employer with two weeks' notice. I like to put in two weeks' notice and take a week off before starting a new job, so I always ask for three weeks notice. I am always willing to start in two weeks. Third, you should never put in notice unless you have a written offer letter. It usually takes a day or two to get your offer package. I will accept an e-mail with the offer terms in place of a formal offer letter for the purposes of putting in my notice. The e-mail should include the job title, start date, and salary information. I know several people who have accepted verbal commitments that did not match what they got when they started. If the company changes your salary, title, or location on your first day, you should quit. If a company is going to back out on commitments, imagine what will happen if you work for them!

Chapter 10
EMPLOYEE AND TEAM MANAGEMENT

There is a perception in popular media that a manager has to be mean to be effective. Plenty of examples on TV include Larry Tate from *Bewitched* and Mr. Spacely from *The Jetsons*. I sometimes think managers feel they need to emulate these stereotypes to be good managers. When I was struggling with my own performance about customer service and supporting the business, I read *How to win friends and Influence People* by Dale Carnegie. He proved to me that you do not need to be mean to be successful, and it is, in fact, counterproductive. Furthermore, you do not need to get something out of being nice to people either; you can be nice just to make someone feel good. I highly recommend Mr. Carnegie's book, and I think everyone should read it.

Caskie Stinnett wrote in his book *Out of the Red,* "A diplomat is a person who can tell you to go to hell in such a way that you actually look forward to the trip." Managers everywhere can learn a lesson from Mr. Stinnett. Once you start a new job, it is very important to develop a good working relationship with your manager and coworkers, and if you are a manager, develop a good working relationship with your employees. Many employees think that if only they were a manager, they would be able to make decisions and tell people what to do. The irony of being a manager is discovering that you actually have less power than you did as an employee. Managers need to keep employees happy, peers happy, and a boss happy.

The First Day
Every employee looks forward to the first day at work. Most of my first days have been either pleasant or off-putting. The good first day starts with the manager meeting you at reception, escorting you to human resources to fill out paperwork, escorting you around the office to meet new coworkers, taking you out to lunch, and giving you a light afternoon. The not so great first day starts when they act surprised you showed up. As the manager, you have a responsibility to get your employees off to a good start.

Once you have an accepted offer letter and a start date, there are several groups you need to coordinate with to make sure your new employee is set up and has a great first day.

- Mark your calendar—I try to keep a new employee's day as free as possible so I can show them around and help them get set up. It does not always work out this way, but I try.
- Human resources—Make sure all the paperwork is ready and someone is available to assist and explain the forms.
- Reception—Let reception know when the new employee will be arriving and the employee's name.
- Security/information security—You may need to get badges, authorization, and other types of access set up for a new employee. Security and/or information security will help you through the process.
- Desktop support—You need to get the new employee a desktop or laptop, a desk, a desk phone, possibly a cell phone.
- Accounts—Set up accounts to access all critical systems and make sure you spell the name correctly.
- Team notification—Send an e-mail to your team letting them know what day the new employee will start.
- Lunch—I love food and everyone has to eat. I like to take new employees out to lunch with the team or one on one depending on your budget. It is a great opportunity to get to know someone outside of work. I try to make first lunches very casual and talk about non-controversial topics. Refer back to the topics you should never talk about and avoid alcohol.
- Putting in time—Hopefully, you will be able to spend most of the employee's first day with them. The relationship does not end after the first day. You need to make a point of communicating with your employees regularly. You should know what they are working on, what they are struggle with, what their career goals are and a little about them. When you neglect your employees, morale will suffer. If you have not been doing this, make a point of showing an interest starting tomorrow!

On your first day as an employee you have it easy, show up, have a positive attitude, fill out your benefits paperwork, and hopefully get a free lunch.

Setting Goals

I like to set expectations with employees and managers as early as possible. I have the same speech for managers and employees. I tell them that I am honest and straightforward and that if there is a problem to come to me directly so we can work it out. I have felt ambushed in the past by a manager, where the first time I found out about a problem was on my performance review. This is unfair because I never had an opportunity to take corrective action. This discussion should happen by the end of the first week at the latest.

When I am the manager, I also like to review the job description again in the first week. Get the job description you wrote approved by human resources and then file it. This reaffirms that everyone knows what is expected. Most managers never bother to take this step, and it leads to frustration and confusion on all sides. I think this is because managers and employees think job responsibilities are obvious. Every time I have reviewed a job description and expectations, there has always been at least one point needing clarification. After that, I like to discuss employee goals, team goals, and company goals. It is important for employee to see where their contributions fit into the big picture at a company. The last thing I like to cover is the career goals of the employee. It is impossible to motivate employees if you do not know what interests them. Once I know what employees are interested in, I try to get them training and projects that relate to their interests.

One on One Meetings

When you are a manager, regularly meet with the members on your team. This gives you a chance to see the progress employees are making on goals for the year, find out any challenges they are facing, and get to know them better. I try to meet with each employee once a week or biweekly for thirty minutes. I have found this gives employees a chance to voice any concerns they have and lets me make sure they are making progress on assigned goals.

Yearly Reviews

Most companies have a policy of yearly reviews that include employee performance, salary raises, possible bonuses, or other recognition. It gives the manager a chance to give employees formal feedback. If performance has been good, provide rewards and bonuses.

The manager should work with human resources to find out how to handle yearly reviews, salary increases, and bonuses. Companies handle yearly reviews for the entire company at the same time or based on hire dates. I prefer to get them all at the same time because I can plan all the salary increases and bonuses just once a year. Senior management approves salary increases and bonuses, usually put into a pool across the company or by department. Three percent is a common increase level across the board. If your department gets a 3 percent increase for the team, you can give everyone a 3 percent raise or give some people more and others less. If employees know the raise percentage across the company, this can create hurt feelings with employees that receive less than the average. I do not recommend sharing the pool-percentage level with the company. I think the best employees deserve good raises and the employees that need the most improvement should get a small or no raise. Performance should be rewarded. I have created a very simple chart showing three employees. If you are really assessing employee raises, create a much more sophisticated chart that captures the full scope of the job employees are doing.

	Employee A	Employee B	Employee C
Performance Review (1 to 5, 5 is best)	5	3	1
Raise percentage (3 percent average)	5 percent	3 percent	1 percent

Team Management

Most of the same tools you use to manage individual employees apply to teams.

Set goals—Teams should have goals just like individual employees. Tie the goals to individual goals and organizational goals. When they achieve milestones, celebrate them just like individual goals.

Face to face—Meet with your team regularly, and if possible, in person. I like to do it weekly whenever possible and keep it short. Even if you are not physically in the same location, I strongly believe in visiting every site and employee you manage. These trips always pay for themselves. You will show the employee they are important to you, build relationships with people onsite and do a site inspection. I also like to travel domestically and internationally, which always worked well for me.

Team meetings—No one really enjoys spending time in meetings, least of all technical people. The shorter and more productive the meeting is, the less resistance you will get. I always publish an agenda in advance, stick to the agenda, hold the meeting consistently at the same time and place, and try not to let the meeting be too serious.

Team building and team outings—These can be a great tool for building teamwork. I recommend steering away from events with alcohol. If you are at an event that serves alcohol and you do not have any medical or religious restrictions, it is polite to have one or two glasses, but avoid having more. I have seen more than one employee embarrass himself or herself drinking, you don't want it to be you.

Yearly Review—Review the successes and challenges of a team with the whole team. It is worth the time to put together a short presentation of the previous year's success and the goals for the upcoming year. Always thank the team for good progress, and work with the team at team meetings for solutions to problems the team is facing. In football, quarterbacks that take all the credit after a big game, end up sacked at the next game. I do not think that is an accident.

Performance Improvement Plans

What do you do when an employee is doing a poor job? Most companies ignore the problem or wait far too long to deal with it. This leads to poor performance across the company and low morale. If you do not deal with performance issues, they will deal with you. Employees that are not performing affect the morale of the people around them, and someone else has to pick up the slack. If you deal with the problem right away, you can sometimes prevent it from becoming a bigger issue later.

I always try to provide positive feedback when I provide constructive criticism. If you are having one-on-one meetings, this is the perfect time to discuss performance. If you have not established weekly meetings, establish them for the whole team. This will avoid making the person feel like he or she is being singled out, and you should be having these meetings anyway. Keep detailed notes of your conversations. If you do not see improvement or you see the same mistakes repeated, you need to move to a performance improvement plan (PIP).

A well-crafted PIP is a team effort between you as the manager, your manager, and human resources. Explain the situation to your manager and human resources to obtain approval to start a PIP. If they agree, fill out a PIP that includes specific details of what the employee did wrong, what actions you took to mentor the employee, the measureable goals you set to gauge the success or failure of the plan, and the time limit you set. I always include at least two goals and no more than four. First, if the employee is the only one who knows how to do something, you should put in the plan that he has to train someone else. Second, require the employee to provide documentation for all job responsibilities. I also recommend a thirty-day time limit because a shorter period is not enough time to make corrections, and anything longer can be difficult to manage.

Performance problems generally fall into two categories: technical and attitude. Technical issues relate to the ability to perform a job function. You can usually solve these problems with additional training or mentoring. Attitude problems relate to poor interpersonal skills, an unwillingness to perform job duties, or simply not showing up. Attitude problems present a bigger challenge. They are hard to improve and difficult to measure. Performance Improvement Plan forms should always state that a failure to improve could lead to action up to and including termination. If performance does not improve, you will usually move on to termination. Review your plan with your manager and human resources to make sure the plan is fair, complies with policies, and addresses the issues objectively and unemotionally. This also shows the company, employee and in any litigation that you were objective in your assessment and actions.

You can meet with the employee by yourself or ask human resources and/or your manager to join you. If you think the employee will be unreceptive to the performance improvement plan, you will definitely want someone else present. Go to the meeting with a copy of the job description, two copies of the performance improvement plan, and a pad and pen to take notes. I review the job description to make sure we both have the same understanding of what the job responsibilities are. I follow that with a history of the concerns and then go through the PIP line by line. Once you have given a brief overview, show the employee the document and go through the issues and required improvements step by step. Once you finish going through the document, give the employee a chance to comment. However, any comments the employee makes should not change the PIP. If the employee makes derogatory, negative comments, or disputes your claims, make a note of them on your pad. Once you end the meeting, you and the employee sign both copies. Give a copy to human resources.

Meet with the employee weekly to discuss any negative or positive improvements you have seen, and send a copy to the employee and human resources. You should be able to tell what direction the plan is going within the first week. If things are improving even in small ways, encourage your employee to continue to make changes and improve. If you do not see improvement, discuss termination with human resources and your manager. If everyone agrees, move forward with termination.

What do you do if you are an employee that receives a performance improvement plan? The circumstances can vary greatly between one situation and another. You need to determine the best course of action for you. If you think you can work with your manager and keep your job, you should try to work with the plan. If you think the Performance Improvement Plan is a formality or you are truly unhappy, start looking for another job. The best way to tell if the PIP is a formality is whether there are clear measureable goals in the plan. If there are no reasonable goals, you will be terminated. If the company does terminate you before you find another job, file for unemployment.

Termination

Terminations are the hardest thing a manager has to do. I always try to remember, that if employees lose their jobs, they could lose their homes, cars, and savings. If firing people does not bother you, I do not recommend being a manager. It is a decision that no one should take lightly. However, you also need to realize that employees have a responsibility to perform their assigned job duties and you have a responsibility to the company. If you have tried to mentor employees, provided a fair performance improvement plans and made an effort to work with employees, you have done all you can.

When you have reached the difficult decision to terminate an employee, you need to get approval from your manager and human resources. If you have done your job, the employee, human resources, and your manager should all be aware of the concerns. There are several steps to terminate an employee.

1.) Arrange the meeting—You need to arrange a meeting to discuss the termination

2.) Plan for covering the employee's responsibilities—You need to know in advance, who will cover the employee's responsibilities once that person leaves. The documentation and training of someone for redundancy noted in the steps of the performance improvement plan should have taken care of this.

3.) Return all equipment—Know what company equipment an employee has and make sure that person returns it. During the meeting, someone should take and secure the employee's laptop or desktop. I do not allow employees to look at a company machine after termination. The computer is company property and the company owns all data. Turn the computer over to information security for analysis and potential legal action. Do not let the desktop team handle this because there are chain-of-custody rules that information security should be aware of.

    4.)   Lock all accounts—You need inform the desktop team and information security team to lock all accounts while the termination is happening.

You should meet the employee with human resources for the termination discussion. When you are in an uncomfortable situation, you will find an urge to talk and explain your decision. This is a bad idea that could get you into trouble for saying something inappropriate or creating grounds for a legal case. I say as little as possible and then turn the meeting over to human resources to discuss benefits and next steps. Once human resources has explained benefits, I ask the employee to return any company property, get any personal possessions from their desk and escort them out of the build. If the employee makes a scene, call security, information security, and human resources to help you escort them from the building. If none of those options is available, you can call the local police to have them escorted off the premises. If the employee has a large number of personal possessions, you can arrange to have them shipped or have them escorted off hours with you and security present. I have seen several terminated employees drag mountains of personal possessions out of the building. I never leave more at the office that can fit in a laptop bag, just in case. It is important to remember that everyone is ultimately expendable, unless you own the company.

Once you have completed the termination, you need to have an immediate meeting with your team to explain what happened. Just like with the employee, you should say as little as possible. I use the term "let go" rather than terminated and ask if there are questions. If employees ask any questions, tell them it was a difficult decision and you are ready to move forward with the team. If you are on a team told about a termination, you should not raise any questions.

Terminations are emotionally draining. They can take several weeks to go from performance improvement plan to termination. The day I terminate an employee, I perform the termination and then do as little as possible the rest of the day. The day will be hard enough. You will not make good decisions anyway.

If you are the terminated employee, you should take notes, accept any paperwork, and file for unemployment benefits. You should never make a scene or accusations. The best option is to say as little as possible. If you think you have a legal case, you should consult several lawyers to see what your legal options are.

Leave on Good Terms

Most employees accept a job at another company and do not experience termination. Once you have an offer, it is time to turn in your notice. Ask to speak with your manager privately, explain that you are giving your notice, give the date of your last day, and thank them for the opportunity. I also give the manager a physical letter and follow up with an e-mail. You should always do your best to leave on good terms. It is the right thing to do, but you also may run into the company or your manager again in the future. Here is a sample letter of resignation.

Dear Mr. Monte,

Unfortunately, I have accepted another opportunity and my last day will be July 23, 2012. I will make every effort to make this a smooth transition for your company and provide documentation for all of my responsibilities. Please let me know whom I can work with to pass on my job responsibilities.

Thank you for the opportunity at Cerebellum Strategies, LLC.

Sincerely,
Former Employee

Chapter 11
ORGANIZATIONAL RELATIONSHIPS

Organizational relationships are the relationships between departments in the same company. I will look at this topic primarily from the information technology point of view, but most of the advice should work for almost any department. The relationships you build with other departments are as important as the ones you build with employees and peers within your department. A good relationship can make it easy to hire new employees, enjoy bigger budgets, and be included in critical decisions the company makes. When the company sees information technology as a partner, you will be able to influence decisions and the direction of information technology.

Business Units

The business units are the departments directly making the business money. If these departments did not exist, the company would not exist. While the business units should have some understanding of information technology, it is critical that information technology understands the tools and processes that are important to the business units. Every employee should know how the company makes money and what its products are. I am a strong believer in requiring technical people to attend training on products and services.

It is impossible for information technology to be effective and efficient, if you do not understand what technology the business relies on to make money. Any technology that is critical to the core business should be the top priority for information technology. Information technology should meet with the business regularly to understand its needs and continuously work to make improvements that enhance the power of these departments. Information technology teams focused on the core business will find that, instead of fighting for budget and recognition, the business will see them as a value rather than a cost center. This is the central theme of the book, and if you learn only one thing, this should be it.

Accounting

Every team should develop a relationship with accounting. Technology teams need hardware, software, and people. All of those things require money and accounting works with management to control the money.

I used to work at a company where every request went through several layers of management all the way to the CIO. The company had a reputation for rejecting purchase requests or taking weeks to approve them. Managers were afraid of looking bad to the CIO, so they scrutinized every purchase request. An email floated around the company about a $30 purchase rejected by the CIO. Technical employees in the company avoided making purchase requests.

I had to make a purchase request on an international project for this company. The initial scope of the project was to replace a router, which would cost about $30,000. The first step I took was to look at the network design and log into the devices to understand how the network worked. I manually collected my own documentation, created my own network diagrams, and compared them with the official versions. What I discovered was the network would need about $500,000 in improvements, and the official documentation was out of date. I gathered information from the monitoring system to support my case. The next step I took was to gather tickets from the ticketing system to get a sense of the business impact of the inefficiencies. I had a good understanding of how the network worked, what I could do to improve it, and a sense of the common problems the internal customers were facing. The next thing I needed to find out was whether there was a business value to making the change. I spoke to several people in the business and the local manager. I found out that it was the number-one growth location in the company—very profitable and growing. Based on this information, I felt I had a good business case to make the changes that I thought the site needed.

Most technical people would send in this request: "I would like to purchase $500,000 in equipment for the branch office." The management at this company would definitely reject a request like this. I wrote my purchase request differently. Here is a sample e-mail similar to what I wrote.

"I would like to purchase $500,000 in equipment for the branch office (see-itemized attachment A). The branch office has been experiencing frequent outages, as noted in the spreadsheet with the attached issues (see attachment B) and screenshots from the monitoring system (see attachment C). The estimated business cost of these outages is $600,000 (see attachment D). If we implement these changes this year, the business will save $100,000 next year.

I also have a solid technical plan for completing the project. I have attached the project plan, before and after network diagrams, and spreadsheets with supporting information.

Thank you for your time."

My request was approved a couple of days later without any questions asked. The other engineers thought I performed a miracle. Why did it work? I did three things. First, I explained to the business the return on investment or ROI. They would spend $500,000 and end up saving $100,000. Who would turn down that deal? Second, I provided detailed documentation supporting my plan. Third, I provided a well-thought-out plan for executing the project that had a good chance of success. If you are asking the company to spend money, you need to explain why they should in terms they will understand. I always view company purchases as if it were my money. If you look at it from that point of view, you will make better decisions and do the right ones for the business.

The job does not stop at getting the funding or even completing the work. I followed through on my plan, received feedback from users, and generated reports from the ticketing system showing the project was successful and the business unit was pleased with my work. This proved the money was well spent and made it even easier to secure funding going forward, because I had built up trust with the business by following through on my promise. You will want to include accounting when you save the company money throughout the process.

You may also deal with accounting on developing budgets. Budgets are different from requesting funds for a project. You should meet with accounting, understand the process, and get a copy of last year's projected and actual budgets. You should also meet with your management. They will help you identify the costs and strategic goals of the company that you need to account for in your budget. Be as detailed as possible within the guidelines of the accounting department. Here is a sample budget.

Item	Cost	Explanation
Employee salaries	$800,000	10 employees
Employee benefits	$200,000	10 employee benefit plans
Cubicles	$100,000	10 employee cubicles
Phones	$2,000	10 employee phones
Laptops	$3,000	Replace 2 laptops
Data Center	$100,000	Data center environmental
Servers	$40,000	New server upgrades and support
Network Hardware	$60,000	Routers, firewalls, switches
Project Cablepolooza	$20,000	Plan to replace cabling
Project Virtualatron	$60,000	Virtualization project
Total	$1,385,000	Budget for 2013

As you can see, employee salaries are a large part of the budget. I have always wanted to work on projects with interesting names. My peers would always shoot down my cool project code names. Fortunately I can add them here with no one to stop me.

There is one thing accounting should hold information technology responsible for. The employee responsible for a service should be required to sign off on all bills for that service. For example, I was responsible for the WAN circuits at this particular company and I had to sign the bill every month before the vendor was paid. It made me responsible the bill was paid and the company got any credits or discounts we negotiated. I found plenty of errors and saved the company a significant amount of money. It also helped me forge a relationship with the accounting team. I highly recommend adding accountability to all processes and I think all companies should adopt this one.

Human Resources

We have already discussed how important a good relationship with human resources is to the hiring, performance improvement, and termination process. Human resources can also play a role in helping employees through personal issues, adoption, smoking cessation, dieting, tuition reimbursement, and company events. Managers and employees should be aware of all the services the company offers.

There is one other situation where you may be working with human resources. Occasionally, an employee will come to a manager with a personal issue such as a divorce, a death in the family, an adoption, an illness, or some other personal matter. I always encourage these employees to speak with human resources to get the support they need. If they need a few extra days off, I give it to them. Employees will appreciate flexibility.

Executive Management

Information technology usually has limited interaction with upper management, but here are a few general guidelines for dealing with executive management. First, they are the ones signing your paycheck, so always give their issues priority, unless there is a bigger issue affecting the business. Second, they are usually very busy with everyone competing for their time. You want to make your interaction direct, objective, and to the point. Third, you want to present solution choices rather problems. I always present viable solutions and the pros and cons of each choice so they can make an informed decision. If there are no viable alternatives, explain the situation at a quick, high level. Fourth, if they ask you for information or a presentation, return it as soon as possible.

If you are a manager involved in deciding raises, it is your job to get as much money for your team as you can. Senior management will usually have a pool of money for raises for the entire company. Make a presentation explaining what your team has done for the company and the effort put in, such as 500 hours of overtime. You want to convince them your team deserves a bigger share of the pool.

Senior Management will get involved in major outage or security breach, the key to successfully resolving the problem and maintaining a good relationship with senior management is communication. As soon as you are aware of the outage, follow these steps:

1.) Assessment—Assess the scope of the problem. It does not do any good to investigate when you do not know the scope of the problem.

Contact the help desk, your team, and any other relevant technology groups to assess the scope. I keep notes in a draft e-mail during the call, then edit, and send it once the issue is resolved.

2.) Document—You should open a ticket with the help desk if there is not one already.

3.) Notification—Call your manager so she can inform senior management, and ask the help desk to contact any employees or clients affected.

4.) Coordinated response—Once you have identified the problem, set up a conference call and provide it to all technical parties involved and to senior management. If the issue affects customers, someone should be responsible for communicating updates to them. The manager should be providing updates to management, making sure the troubleshooting process is systematic, and making sure senior management gives the team time to resolve the problem. These situations sometimes heat up, particularly if the parties believe human error is the cause. However, you should remind everyone to focus on fixing the problem. The team can sort out the root cause after the problem is resolved. If you can deflect discussion unrelated to solving the problem until after the call, the issue will resolve that much faster.

5.) Regular updates—Most companies follow the first four steps, but technology teams tend to forget to provide regular updates to management or the ticket. You should schedule updates at least every hour. The worst thing you can do is provide no update because even if you are working on the issue, the appearance is that you are not. The regular updates also help keep the troubleshooting process on task, because you know you need to report back to management and possibly customers.

6.) Root cause identified—Once you identify the root cause of the issue, send out a status update, even if it doesn't happen when you already have a regular update planned.

7.) Solution options—Some problems only have one reasonable solution, but others may have several options. You should always choose the most conservative solution to get the system running again. If you have to chose between a stop gap and extending the outage with a risky long term solution, chose the stop gap and schedule a maintenance window. If you aren't sure which technical option is best, discuss it with the experts to get there advice. If all options carry a high level of risk, present the options to management for a decision.

8.) Resolution—Once you put the resolution in place, and it has proven to be successful for a short period of time, send out another update.

9.) Root cause analysis—Every major incident has a root cause. For example, a server could crash, which causes an incident. The root cause is the server ran out of disk space. The root cause analysis would look at how to prevent the server from running out of space in the future. Most companies don't take this step, it will reduce incidents and create greater stability so the information technology can focus efforts on proactive efforts. It forces a company to understand and deal with the underlying issues of your business and provide long term solutions rather than focusing on band aid fixes.

10.) Regulatory notification requirements—In the case of a security breach, you may legally be required to notify the government or clients. The information security team should be able to manage the process. You will need to work with information security, audit and your legal department to comply with requirements.

Obviously, the best situation is to avoid the outage all together, but if it does happen, the next best thing is to manage the outage professionally and make every effort to avoid those issues in the future.

Senior management will often involve information technology when the company is starting a new project or releasing a new product. I have found that most companies spend a great deal of time planning and coordinating a project, but not much time determining the profitability of a new project or product, particularly when considering information technology costs. It does not make any sense to release a product for sale at $14.95, when it costs information technology $20 to provide the service. Information technology managers should make every effort to make a reasonable estimate on what it will cost information technology to provide a service; otherwise, it sets up the company for failure.

This chapter should give you some ideas with how information technology interacts with the company and what you can do to improve those relationships. The two most important messages in this chapter are to communicate, understand your business, and look at how you can apply technology to meet the strategic goals of the business.

Chapter 12
Conclusion

The goal of this book was to examine the relationships within a company between information technology and the business. There were several steps to exploring the relationship. First, we set out to understand information technology teams. Chapters two through seven discussed each team, what was important to them, and the challenges they face. Although, we did not walk a mile in those team's shoes, we at least tried the shoes on. The purpose of these chapters was to get an understanding of the different groups in information technology. Second, we discussed managing information technology departments, project management, hiring, and employee and team management. Third, we discussed how to build successful relationships in the chapter on organizational relationships. Each of these pieces is critical to understanding and building relationships inside a company.

If we boil the message of the book down even further, it was about providing a good customer experience though understanding and communication. Understanding involves having a high-level view of how businesses work. The more you understand about how a business works the better your decisions will be. Communication was the other major underlying theme. Once you understand, you can take those tools to present your message. You can communicate effectively by communicating problems, solutions and seeking agreement with the people you are working with. Decisions made in a vacuum end poorly for everyone involved. The entire book has recommendations on how to communicate effectively, particularly the chapters on hiring, employee and team management, and organizational relationships.

I hope you enjoyed this book and that it taught you something about business and technology. Thank you for reading.

ABOUT THE AUTHOR

Thomas Monte started working in information technology in 1995. Thomas has since worked all over the world in roles, such as server administrator, network engineer, security analyst, and director of information technology and director of network engineering. Thomas holds certifications as a CISSP, PMP, and ITIL foundations version 3. Thomas posts on his blog http://www.cerebellumstrategies.com or you can e-mail Thomas at tmonte@cerebellumstrategies.com.

(Endnotes)

1 George Santayana, *Reason in Common Sense*, volume 1 of The Life of Reason (1905)

www.ingramcontent.com/pod-product-compliance
Lightning Source LLC
Chambersburg PA
CBHW061020050326
40689CB00012B/2689